# NEW DIRECTIONS FOR HIGHER EDUCATION

Martin Kramer, *University of California, Berkeley*
*EDITOR-IN-CHIEF*

# An Agenda for the New Decade

Larry W. Jones
*Moorehead State University*

Franz A. Nowotny
*Fitchburg State College*

*EDITORS*

Number 70, Summer 1990

JOSSEY-BASS INC., PUBLISHERS
San Francisco • Oxford

An Agenda for the New Decade.
*Larry W. Jones, Franz A. Nowotny (eds.).*
New Directions for Higher Education, no. 70.
Volume XVIII, number 2.

NEW DIRECTIONS FOR HIGHER EDUCATION
*Martin Kramer,* Editor-in-Chief

NEW DIRECTIONS FOR HIGHER EDUCATION is part of The Jossey-Bass Higher Education Series and is published quarterly by Jossey-Bass Inc., Publishers (publication number USPS 990-880). Second-class postage paid at San Francisco, California, and at additional mailing offices. Postmaster: Send address changes to Jossey-Bass Inc., Publishers, 350 Sansome Street, San Francisco, California 94104.

EDITORIAL CORRESPONDENCE should be sent to the Editor-in-Chief, Martin Kramer, 2807 Shasta Road, Berkeley, California 94708.

Library of Congress Catalog Card Number LC 85-644752

International Standard Serial Number ISSN 0271-0560

International Standard Book Number ISBN 1-55542-827-4

Cover photograph and random dot by Richard Blair/Color & Light © 1990. Manufactured in the United States of America. Printed on acid-free paper.

It is with sorrow that we share the sad news that Dr. Larry Jones passed away in March of 1990. We wish to recognize Dr. Jones's career and contribution to higher education through this volume.

—Martin Kramer, Editor-in-Chief
Franz A. Nowotny, Editor

# CONTENTS

# EDITORS' NOTES

This volume offers observations, predictions, and advice on the major issues that will confront colleges and universities during the 1990s from the perspective of several authorities on higher education.

What is going to happen in higher education in general during the 1990s is a key concern to all of us involved in college and university life. In the opening chapter, Clark Kerr examines where we stand today and the kinds of changes we likely will see over the course of the decade.

In Chapter Two, Thomas M. Stauffer presents a view of the twentieth century as the most prolific incubator of new institutional formats. Specifically, partnerships between universities, businesses, and industries have proved a viable institutional strategy for economic and cultural development. The author reviews and catalogues a number of these partnerships and examines how such broadly based development might well become institutionalized as a fourth function of universities, after teaching, research, and community service. Stauffer also thinks a new university model will arise to promote regional dynamism and development.

In Chapter Three, Richard P. Chait, in accord with Clark Kerr, postulates that the 1990s will be the decade of the trustees. He sees a number of developing trends that are likely to increase the influence of the governing boards of universities and colleges. The environment of higher education in the 1990s is likely to be turbulent owing to a variety of social, economic, and political factors and will require boards that are vigilant, informed, and responsive to the needs of administrative officials. Chait sees issues arising around program assessment, constituency relations, and institutional productivity. He asserts that students and faculty will want more direct access to trustees and the role of trustees will become more crucial as fund raising assumes greater significance in an era of declining support from the states.

Jack H. Schuster, in Chapter Four, explores issues that will most affect faculty in the 1990s. He sees this decade as a time of major change for faculty, with far-reaching implications for higher education. Included among the issues discussed are supply and demand, as the composition of existing faculty is altered through the joint processes of retirement of older staff and advancement of much younger people, and faculty salaries, status, and morale. Overall, changes in the marketplace suggest that competition will become intense for quality faculty, creating a situation far more fluid and dynamic than ever before experienced in the academic labor market.

As Frederic Jacobs notes in Chapter Five, a great deal of attention has been given to the faculty work force of the 1990s. Faculty work loads and expectations about productivity are being scrutinized and dramatic changes are underway in these areas. He points out that while faculty activities such as the traditional requirements of teaching, research, and service will remain unchanged, the 1990s will bring a transformation in the relationship between faculty and external agencies and organizations. Three trends are particularly important: greater diversity in instructional assignments, increased requirements for compliance and documentation of activities, and enhanced relationships with the business community, including continuing professional education and assessment of prior learning.

In Chapter Six, Larry W. Jones notes that strategic planning in higher education did not live up to expectations during the 1980s. This failure occurred for a number of reasons, foremost among them being a lack of leadership from presidents and other senior administrative officers, a too diffuse focus in expectations, and an inadequate assessment of the diversity of environments in which institutions of higher learning function. He points out that the 1990s hold hope for strategic planning if chief executive officers spearhead the effort and if the planners engage experienced consultants, utilize proven planning models, and learn to do the "right" things. The author also views leadership, communication, involvement training, timing, and concern for the individual as well as for the organization as necessary to the success of strategic planning.

The thesis that higher education needs to increase quality and productivity and decrease costs for the 1990s is developed by Ellen Earle Chaffee in Chapter Seven. She sees these strategies as the key to effective postsecondary education. Specifically, students, faculty, and dollars must be organized in ways that empower individuals to effect change. The author proposes a variety of such routes to improved postsecondary education.

Women have aspirations to move up within the administrative structure of higher education. Jean Wilson argues in Chapter Eight that women in higher education will experience fewer and less formidable barriers in the 1990s. It is her contention that primary benefits will accrue to those who are now initially obtaining employment in higher education, with somewhat lesser benefits going to those who are already within the academy. The key developments in higher education will include a greater number of women entering the ranks of college faculty and a more positive environment for women who want to enter administrative positions.

In the last chapter, Kenneth P. Mortimer and Sheila R. Edwards examine the college or university president's view of the 1990s. They see three external forces influencing campus presidents and the higher education community during the decade: accountability to the public and the need for campus autonomy, concern about the quality of higher education, and the tendency to talk about access and quality as though the two factors constitute a trade-off. As Mortimer and Edwards argue, leadership from presidents is the key to meeting the challenges wrought from these three forces. A new frontier exists for higher education as its leaders work to define the limits and nature of the involvement with external groups.

While no one can predict with certainty what the next ten years will bring for institutions of higher learning, the authors in this volume have focused on some of the key issues that will confront students, faculty, and administrators over the course of the decade.

Larry W. Jones[†]
Franz A. Nowotny
Editors

*Larry W. Jones was dean of Professional Studies at Moorehead State University, Moorehead, Kentucky.*

*Franz A. Nowotny is associate vice-president of Academic Affairs and dean of graduate studies at Fitchburg State College, Fitchburg, Massachusetts.*

*The 1990s will be a decade of major changes and conflicts, the scenarios of which are rooted in history, often external in origin, and sometimes beyond direct control of higher education.*

# Higher Education Cannot Escape History: The 1990s

*Clark Kerr*

Looking back at the history of higher education in the United States in the twentieth century, at least five observations are well founded:

1. Each decade has had its own characteristics. ✓
2. It would not have been possible to predict these characteristics.
3. These characteristics were more shaped by what was happening outside the academy than inside, that is, higher education was mostly not in control of its own fate.
4. Each succeeding generation within higher education nevertheless has sought to predict and plan for the future, as ideally envisioned.
5. Higher education, regardless of its powers of divination, survived each successive wave of challenges and expanded on a secular basis in size and function.

Now we confront the 1990s, and again, in the words of Abraham Lincoln, "We cannot escape history." And this history may very well include, in an elevated fashion over the 1980s, at least two of the same historical issues with which Lincoln was concerned: race relations and higher education's contributions to the economy (for Lincoln, the land-grant movement.)

The 1980s almost certainly will not be replicated. To expect that they will, I believe, is to live with illusions. The 1980s were a nonhistorical decade—nonhistorical in the sense that so little happened that made history. It was a status quo decade. Enrollments were static. Indeed, as indicated in Table 1, the percentage increase in enrollments was the smallest

NEW DIRECTIONS FOR HIGHER EDUCATION, no. 70, Summer 1990 ©Jossey-Bass Inc., Publishers

**Table 1. Percentage Increases in U.S. University and College Enrollments During the Twentieth Century, by Decade**

| Decade | Percentage Increase |
| --- | --- |
| 1900–1910 | 49 |
| 1910–1920 | 68 |
| 1920–1930 | 84 |
| 1930–1940 | 36 |
| 1940–1950 | 78 |
| 1950–1960 | 31 |
| 1960–1970 | 140 |
| 1970–1980 | 40 |
| 1980–1990 | 6 |
| 1990–2000 | — |

*Source:* Kerr, in press.

thus far in the twentieth century. Financing was static. Academic programs were static and much else, as Table 2 reveals. 1989 was mostly a replica of 1979. Few important decisions were made because few important decisions needed to be made. Decision makers had a mostly free ride. To the extent that presidents make a difference, they make less of a difference in a decade such as the 1980s (Commission on Strengthening Presidential Leadership, 1984). They make more of a difference in times of greater change and greater conflict, and thus, perhaps, they will be more influential once again in the 1990s. The same can also be said of other decision-making entities, including boards of trustees, faculty senates, coordinating mechanisms, and governors. They all had a free ride in the 1980s but may not in the 1990s.

The 1980s were roughly similar, with respect to an easy ride for governing mechanisms, to two other decades in the twentieth century: 1900–1910 and 1920–1930. Both of these decades were also periods of "normalcy."

The 1990s will, I believe, fall into a second category of decades with substantial challenges and changes, along with the other decades in the twentieth century:

1910–1920—World War I: women's suffrage movement on campus; economic depression and period of political reaction after World War I
1930–1940—The Great Depression: student movements, including for peace, for trade unions, for socialism, and for communism
1940–1950—World War II: GI rush at the end of the war; McCarthy period after the war
1950–1960—Korean War: preparations for the tidal wave of students, including expansion plans for the community colleges and transformational plans for the state teachers' colleges

**Table 2. Changing Dimensions of American Higher Education in the 1980s**

| Dimension | 1980 | Change in 1980s | | Late 1980s[a] |
|---|---|---|---|---|
| **Enrollments** | | | | |
| Enrollments | 12 mil. | +.8 mil. | = | 12.8 mil. |
| Enrollments in public institutions | 9.5 mil. | +.5 mil. | = | 10 mil. |
| Enrollments in private institutions | 2.5 mil. | +.3 mil. | = | 2.8 mil. |
| Women as percentage of total enrollment | 51 | +2.5 | = | 53.5 |
| Minorities as percentage of total enrollment | 17 | +1.4 | = | 18.4 |
| Percentage of blacks aged 20 and 21 enrolled in school or college | 23 | +2.7 | = | 25.7 |
| Percentage of whites aged 20 and 21 enrolled in school or college | 32 | +1.5 | = | 33.5 |
| Percentage of freshmen intending to major in business or engineering | 36 | 0 | = | 36 |
| **Degrees** | | | | |
| Number of doctoral degrees conferred | 33,000 | +1,000 | = | 34,000/yr. |
| Number of medical doctor degrees conferred | 15,000 | +600 | = | 15,600/yr. |
| **Faculty** | | | | |
| Size of professoriat | 685,000 | +41,000 | = | 726,000 |
| Number of faculty covered by collective bargaining agreements | 190,000 (1985) | +37,000 | = | 227,000 |
| **Institutions** | | | | |
| Number of institutions | 3,200 | +400 | = | 3,600 |
| Number of public institutions | 1,500 | +100 | = | 1,600 |
| Number of private institutions | 1,700 | +300 | = | 2,000 |
| Enrollment in public institutions as percentage of total | 80 | 0 | = | 80 |

*Source:* Based on Kerr, in press.

[a]Dates vary; 1986 to 1989 as available.

**Table 2.** *(continued)*

| Dimension | 1980 | Change in 1980s | | Late 1980s[a] |
|---|---|---|---|---|
| Percentage of public enrollment in community colleges and comprehensive colleges and universities | 70 | 0 | = | 70 |
| Enrollment in community colleges | 4 mil. | +.5 mil. | = | 4.5 mil. |
| Enrollment in public comprehensive colleges and universities | 2.4 mil. | +.1 mil. | = | 2.5 mil. |
| Federal and state support | | | | |
| Federal research and development to universities (1980 $) | $4,300 mil. | +1,400 mil. | = | $5,700 mil. |
| Federal student aid (1980 $) | $10 bil. | +$1 bil. | = | $11 bil. |
| State expenditures on operations of higher education institutions (1980 $) | $21 bil. | +$4.5 bil. | = | $25.5 bil. |
| Other indicators | | | | |
| Percentage of students in public institutions in states with coordinating mechanisms and/or consolidated governing boards | 94 | 0 | = | 94 |
| Number of states with coordinating mechanisms and/or consolidated governing boards | 46 | 0 | = | 46 |
| States with universal access to higher education | 50 | 0 | = | 50 |
| Estimated accumulated student years in higher education | 220 mil. | +80 mil. | = | 300 mil. |

*Source:* Based on Kerr, in press.

[a]Dates vary; 1986 to 1989 as available.

Two other decades, 1960-1970 and 1970-1980, were decades of transformation (see Table 3).

For an impressionistic view of the decades, see Table 4. As it indicates, a decade with at least major changes or conflicts is the norm.

## Alternative Scenarios

The process of building scenarios is already well underway for the 1990s. At least three cautions are needed as this process moves along: (1) Many scenarios look mostly at a single major aspect of the possible future and not at how these several possible aspects may interact and at what comparative weight should be given to each. (2) No scenarios can adequately be prepared for the unforeseen. And yet the unforeseen has written much of the recent history of higher education. The tidal wave of students of the 1960s was foreseen but not the nationwide racial revolt, not the Vietnam War, not the consequent student unrest, not the OPEC crises of the 1970s, and not the failure of the demographic depression of the 1980s to put in its widely promised appearance. Take out these unforeseen developments and you take out much of the history of the past thirty years. (3) Some scenarios are "hope for" scenarios and some are "will be" scenarios.

**Scenario 1: Driving the Money Changers Out of the Temple.** Colleges and universities inherited a protected status as descendants of the churches from which they originally evolved, and they maintained this status as a result of their own high standards of conduct. This status, however, is now under attack as never before, partly because of the national mood of distrust that followed the scandals of Iran-Contra, Ivan Boesky, and the Savings and Loans industry, and partly because of the conduct of colleges and universities in the areas of athletics, rising tuitions, alleged misconduct in scientific research, and denial of free speech on campus to unpopular speakers, among others. Illustrative of the many attacks is Sykes (1988), who examines a profession "run amok." The universities "will be saved" not by themselves but rather by legislators, governors, parents and students, and perhaps even some trustees, all united in revolts against fraudulent practices. The charges in Sykes's indictment are true, but each to only a very small degree. Depicting these many small degrees as though they were the totality of reality creates, overall, a totally false impression. Nevertheless, the impression is gaining widespread acceptance. Colleges and universities are falling from grace. But falling from grace is a long way off from a united revolt. The chances of a Holy War of purification against the "den of robbers" seem remote, however strongly supported by some critics.

**Scenario 2: Restoring Quality in General and the Centrality of Liberal Education in Particular.** This is the theme of Mayhew, Ford, and Hubbard (1980), among others. More attention must be devoted to the "basics," as

**Table 3.  Changing Dimensions of American Higher Education, 1960-1980**

| Dimension | 1960 | Change to 1980 | | 1980 |
|---|---|---|---|---|
| Enrollments | | | | |
| Enrollments | 3.5 mil. | +8.5 mil. | = | 12 mil. |
| Enrollments in public institutions | 2 mil. | +7.5 mil. | = | 9.5 mil. |
| Enrollments in private institutions | 1.5 mil. | +1 mil. | = | 2.5 mil. |
| Women as percentage of total enrollment | 37 | +14 | = | 51 |
| Minorities as percentage of total enrollment | 10 (1968) | +7 | = | 17 |
| Percentage of blacks aged 20 and 21 enrolled in school or college | 12 | +11 | = | 23 |
| Percentage of whites aged 20 and 21 enrolled in school or college | 21 | +11 | = | 32 |
| Percentage of undergraduate enrollment in professional programs | 38 (1969) | +20 | = | 58 (1976) |
| Degrees | | | | |
| Number of doctoral degrees conferred | 10,000 | +23,000 | = | 33,000/yr. |
| Number of medical doctor degrees conferred | 7,000 | +8,000 | = | 15,000/yr. |
| Faculty | | | | |
| Size of professoriat | 235,000 | +450,000 | = | 685,000 |
| Number of faculty covered by collective bargaining agreements | 0 | +190,000 | = | 190,000 (1985) |
| Institutions | | | | |
| Number of institutions | 2,000 | +1,200 | = | 3,200 |
| Number of public institutions | 700 | +800 | = | 1,500 |
| Number of private institutions | 1,300 | +400 | = | 1,700 |
| Enrollment in public institutions as percentage of total | 60 | +20 | = | 80 |

**Table 3.** (continued)

| Dimension | 1960 | Change to 1980 | | 1980 |
|---|---|---|---|---|
| Percentage of public enrollment in community colleges and comprehensive colleges and universities | 50 | +20 | = | 70 |
| Enrollment in community colleges | 400,000 | +3,600,000 | = | 4 mil. |
| Enrollment in public comprehensive colleges and universities | 600,000 | +1,800,000 | = | 2.4 mil. |
| Federal and state support | | | | |
| Federal research and development to universities (1980 $) | $1,300 mil. | +3,000 mil. | = | $4,300 mil. |
| Federal student aid (1980 $) | $300 mil. | +$9.7 bil. | = | $10 bil. |
| State expenditures on operations of higher education institutions (1980 $) | $4 bil. | +$17 bil. | = | $21 bil. |
| Other indicators | | | | |
| Percentage of students in public institutions in states with coordinating mechanisms and/or consolidated governing boards | 42 | +52 | = | 94 |
| Number of states with coordinating mechanisms and/or consolidated governing boards | 21 | +25 | = | 46 |
| States with universal access to higher education | 1 | +49 | = | 50 |
| Estimated accumulated student years in higher education | 75 mil. | +145 mil. | = | 220 mil. |

*Source:* Based on Kerr, in press.

**Table 4. Change or Conflict in U.S. Universities and
Colleges During the Twentieth Century, by Decade**

| Decade | Change and/or Conflict |
|---|---|
| 1900–1910 | Minor |
| 1910–1920 | Major |
| 1920–1930 | Minor |
| 1930–1940 | Major |
| 1940–1950 | Major |
| 1950–1960 | Major |
| 1960–1970 | Transformational |
| 1970–1980 | Transformational |
| 1980–1990 | Minor |
| 1990–2000 | Major (anticipated) |

many observers, including me, agree. But the many who agree do not
include most students of today, or most faculty members. The students,
instead, are flocking to the professions (the proportion of enrollments in
the arts and sciences has dropped by one-half in recent times), and faculty
members, by and large, are pursuing what Bertrand Russell once called the
"fiercer specializations," even in the humanities. The dire rhetoric of tomes
on the best-seller lists is not being matched by action at ground level (see,
for example, Bloom, 1987).

**Scenario 3: The Coming Racial Crisis in American Higher Education.**
This crisis will be a prominent feature of the 1990s as seen, for example,
by Altbach and Lomotey (forthcoming). Different racial cultures are "living
separately, with little knowledge of, or respect for, each other"; and there
are "flashpoints of crisis." The trend line of racial incidents on campus is
rising. What was once de jure separate but equal has now become de facto
equal but separate. At the minimum, there will be many demographic
realities and opportunities to contend with over the course of the 1990s
(see Levine and others, 1989). The size of the likely college-going population, both young and old, will be smaller, and the population will be
composed mostly of persons who are less adequately prepared academically, less likely to complete the studies needed to receive a degree, and
more likely to require remedial education, financial assistance, and academic, occupational, and personal counseling. However, I do not believe
that "these realities point to a period of adversity for colleges and universities as bad as any in the memory of those living today" (Altbach and
Lomotey, forthcoming). Those still living today include persons who remember the 1960s and 1970s. One of the greatest opportunities of the decade,
nevertheless, will be the consideration given by higher education to the
welfare of what have historically been the "underserved" elements of youth
from low-income families and underrepresented minorities.

**Scenario 4: The Barricades Rising Once More.** "Barricades" are the
theme of Whalen and Flacks (1989). Student revolts have been recurrent in

the history of American higher education since the early years of Harvard. By the middle 1990s, the last such major revolt will be thirty years in the past; and the revolt prior to that was yet another thirty years earlier in the 1930s. The "revolutionary commitment" of the veterans of the 1960s still exists (some of these individuals are now faculty members), and "the spirit waits for a new opportunity that will permit the tide of collective action once more to rise" (Whalen and Flacks, 1989, p. 283). (It has been suggested that the spirit may not have long to wait; see Charney, 1989, p. 9.) But student bodies (and faculties) are now divided over race, not united by opposition to racial injustice and the Vietnam War; and there are no foreign utopias or leaders to inspire and to emulate—not Cuba, not China, not North Vietnam, and not the USSR; and no Che Guevara, no Mao, no Ho Chi Minh, and no Lenin and his vanguard elite. Additionally, low-cohort generations of students historically have been more satisfied and more passive (as the generation of the 1990s may be) than high-cohort generations, which tend to be more dissatisfied and more aggressive (as in the 1960s; see Easterlin, 1978).

**Scenario 5: The Increasing Deficits of Ph.D.s.** Demand for new faculty will rise faster than supply as faculty members employed in the 1960s begin to retire and as enrollments start to rise again; and the deficits will be substantial. This scenario is the well-argued expectation of Bowen and Sosa (1989) for the arts and sciences. But the much greater crisis at the time of the "tidal wave" of students in the 1960s was handled without substantial damage. Also, as Bowen and Sosa note, there are many processes of adjustment: higher student-faculty ratios, more part-time and short-term appointments including those without doctoral degrees, more entrants into Ph.D. programs, shorter periods to completion of the degree, lower quit rates and later retirements by existing faculty, and more recruits from abroad (doctoral awards in the sciences reached an all-time record high in 1988).

**Scenario 6: American Professors as an Endangered Species.** Bowen and Schuster (1986, p. 269) see a "dangerous but not yet desperate situation." Real salary levels have fallen behind national trends, the quality of student preparation has gone down, the faculty has fragmented, bureaucratic controls have increased, more faculty members are part time and short term, the quality of physical facilities has deteriorated, fewer of the ablest young people are attracted into the profession, faculty morale has declined, and much else has gone wrong. But the campus still provides an attractive way of life, most faculty members are satisfied or even very satisfied with their source of employment, and, under the conditions of the 1990s, faculty salaries will rise faster and promotions will come sooner in many fields. It should be a comparatively good decade for the professoriat. A recent survey (Carnegie Foundation for the Advancement of Teaching, 1989, p. 44) found that "faculty are increasingly optimistic about their own profession."

Scenario 7: The Accelerating Internationalization of Academic Life. This will be the great theme for Western Europe in the 1990s, but also a theme for the United States. More students and faculty members will be exchanged among nations. More attention will be paid to world history and to cultures around the globe. Academia is becoming "one world," as banking already has. The 1990s will be a great decade for global perspectives in education. But a great decade additionally is expected for the biological sciences, and also for the professions of engineering, health care, and teaching.

## A Possible Composite Scenario

My own composite scenario, which draws on several of the above-outlined scenarios and on the other chapters of this volume, is as follows:

1. The struggle between equality of opportunity based on merit versus equality of results based on numerical proportionality will intensify. It will be over admissions policies for students at all levels, but particularly also over diversity in the faculty to reflect the new diversity in the student body. Heavy hiring of new faculty members over the next decade and into the early years of the new century creates a context within which struggles over selection of new appointments will go on at the department, school, and college levels as never before in American history. All of these little struggles may add up to some big struggles. And both the little and big struggles will set faculty member against faculty member and student against student. Already there have been signs of a backlash among Euro-American and Asian-American students who feel they have been paying and will continue to pay the costs of affirmative action. (See, for example, the discussion by Auerbach, 1988. What was once "silent opposition" is now becoming more vocal.)

2. The push by national economic and political leaders for higher education to make a greater contribution to U.S. industrial competitiveness will also intensify, leading to more and better skills training and more and better research, particularly in applied areas. This push is particularly strong at the gubernatorial level. I am convinced that the expectations for affirmative results are higher than the potential ability of higher education to fulfill them within a relatively short time frame; and this can lead to disappointments. The push is in the direction of greater emphasis on merit and more compensatory equality of opportunity (such as Head Start), and away from equality of results via numerical proportionality. Higher education will be caught in a vise between strong insistence on both competency and proportionality.

3. The battle for a place in the academic sun will become more fierce, particularly among the research universities. In a period of fifteen years, when there may be a 75 percent turnover in the faculty, the chances that some universities will do better than others in the recruitment battles are

very high. The historical hierarchy of prestige may be shaken up as seldom if ever before—who will win and who will lose?

4. Additional financial resources will be in high demand to advance equality of opportunity, to support competency, and to finance competitive recruiting. Also, physical plants and equipment have been getting older (nearly one-third of the physical plants in academia were built in the 1960s) and often have been poorly maintained. It has been estimated that renovation and replacement will cost $60 billion at current prices against a total investment in physical capital at a replacement cost of $300 billion (Rush and Johnson, 1989; Kaiser, 1984). Additionally, the costs of higher education rise faster than those of the economy as a whole, since they are not easily offset by increased productivity and historically have not been offset at all. Where will the money come from? In the 1960s, productivity was rising at a rate of 3 percent a year, now it is at 1.5 percent. In the 1960s, the nation was the greatest creditor in the history of the world, now it is the greatest debtor. The competition for resources will be ferocious for preschool, primary, and secondary education, for paying off the federal debt, for modernizing the physical infrastructure of the nation, for strengthening the social infrastructure, for supporting economic and political reform around the world, and for much else. And, in the 1960s, the big investment made in higher education was clearly supported by vast increases in student enrollments, but this will not be so in the 1990s. And what if there should be a series of recessions as in the 1970s? Regardless of the overall consequences for higher education, all institutions will not fare equally. The most vulnerable institutions are likely to be the less selective liberal arts colleges, for these are the institutions that provide much of the diversity within American higher education and that have been so instrumental in introducing underrepresented elements of the population to advanced education, for example, African-Americans, Catholics, and Protestant Fundamentalists.

5. Higher education will need to put more effort both into rebuilding the public trust that has eroded over the past thirty years as scandals and complaints have accumulated and into resisting increased external coordination and control. The two tasks go together but so too do the forces that encourage outside interference in what have previously been internal affairs. Specifically, there will be greater public concern for participation by minorities, for attention to conservation of resources within higher education, for rising costs of attending college, for attention to teaching, for emphasis on the basics and on liberal education, for contributions to advancement of the economy, for improved teacher education and other assistance to the high schools, and for much else. At present, the burden of these concerns has been carried mostly by the states and, within the states, by the governors. A draft report titled "Higher Education Agenda" (Education Commission of the States, 1989) states the following:

[W]e sense a growing frustration—even anger—among many of the nation's governors, state legislators, and major corporate leaders that higher education is seemingly disengaged from the battle. Colleges and universities are perceived more often than not as the source of the problems rather than part of the solution. The issues raised are usually specific: lack of involvement in solutions to the problems of urban schools, failure to lead in the reform of teacher education, questions about faculty work load and productivity and lack of commitment to teaching or the escalating and seemingly uncontrollable cost of a college education. But whatever the issue, the overall sense of many outside of colleges and universities is either that dramatic action will be needed to shake higher education from its internal lethargy and focus, or that the system must be bypassed for other institutional forms and alternatives.

6. A place must be reserved for as yet unforeseen events, much as there have been surprises in past decades for higher education.

7. There will be rising pressure, compared with the 1980s, on decision-making processes within higher education, particularly at the levels of trustees, presidents, and faculty senates. Some existing peril points in the structures of governance may well show up (see Commission on Strengthening Presidential Leadership, 1984; Kerr and Gade, 1986, 1989).

It will not be easy to reconcile merit versus proportionality, to meet the demand for saving the economy, to face the competition in the recruitment of a whole new generation of faculty members, to secure additional resources, to restore public trust, to fend off attacks on autonomy, to be ready to handle surprises, and to review and improve decision-making processes.

The 1990s will likely be another decade, among several in this century, marked by major changes and conflicts. And higher education once again will survive and grow in size and in complexity of functions.

## References

Altbach, P. G., and Lomotey, K. (eds.). *The Racial Crisis in American Education.* Albany: State University of New York Press, in press.

Auerbach, C. A. "The Silent Opposition of Professors and Graduate Students to Preferential Affirmative Action Programs: 1969 and 1975." *Minnesota Law Review,* 1988, 72 (6), 1233–1280.

Bloom, A. *The Closing of the American Mind.* New York: Simon and Schuster, 1987.

Bowen, H. R., and Schuster, J. H. *American Professors: A National Resource Imperiled.* New York: Oxford University Press, 1986.

Bowen, W. G., and Sosa, J. A. *Prospects for Faculty in the Arts and Sciences: A Study of Factors Affecting Demand and Supply, 1987 to 2012.* Princeton, N.J.: Princeton University Press, 1989.

Carnegie Foundation for the Advancement of Teaching. *The Condition of the Profes-*

soriate—Attitudes and Trends. Princeton, N.J.: Carnegie Foundation for the Advancement of Teaching, 1989.

Charney, C. "Rebels with a Cause." Times Higher Education Supplement, no. 882, September 29, 1989.

Commission on Strengthening Presidential Leadership (Clark Kerr, chair). Presidents Make a Difference. Washington, D.C.: Association of Governing Boards of Universities and Colleges, 1984.

Easterlin, R. A. "What Will 1984 Be Like? Socioeconomic Implications of Recent Twists in Age Structure." Demography, 1978, 15 (4), 397-432.

Education Commission of the States. "Higher Education Agenda." Unpublished report, Denver, Co., August 1989.

Kaiser, H. H. Crumbling Academe: Solving the Capital Renewal and Replacement Dilemma. Washington, D.C.: Association of Governing Boards of Universities and Colleges, 1984.

Kerr, C. "Prologue." In Commentaries on the Great Transformations in Higher Education, 1960-1980. Albany: State University of New York Press, in press.

Kerr, C., and Gade, M. L. The Many Lives of Academic Presidents: Time, Place, and Character. Washington, D.C.: Association of Governing Boards of Universities and Colleges, 1986.

Kerr, C., and Gade, M. L. The Guardians: Boards of Trustees of American Colleges and Universities. Washington, D.C.: Association of Governing Boards of Universities and Colleges, 1989.

Levine, A., and Associates. Sharing Higher Education's Future: Demographic Realities and Opportunities, 1990-2000. San Francisco: Jossey-Bass, 1989.

Mayhew, L. B., Ford, P. J., and Hubbard, D. L. Surviving the Nineties: Restoring Quality to Undergraduate Education. San Francisco: Jossey-Bass, 1990.

Rush, S. C., and Johnson, S. L. The Decaying American Campus: A Ticking Time Bomb. Washington, D.C.: Association of Physical Plant Administrators of Universities and Colleges and the National Association of College and University Business Officers (in cooperation with Coopers & Lybrand), 1989.

Sykes, C. J. Profscam: Professors and the Demise of Higher Education. Washington, D.C.: Regnery Gateway, 1988.

Whalen, J., and Flacks, R. Beyond the Barricades: The Sixties Generation Grows Up. Philadelphia: Temple University Press, 1989.

Clark Kerr is president emeritus of the University of California. Among his many past service achievements are chair of the Carnegie Council on Policy Studies in Higher Education from 1974 to 1980, president of the University of California from 1958 to 1967, and membership on President Eisenhower's Commission on National Goals and on the Committee on Labor Management Policy under presidents Kennedy and Johnson.

*Economic demands on postsecondary education in this decade will boost the formation of partnership universities for regional economic and cultural development.*

# A University Model for the 1990s

*Thomas M. Stauffer*

American colleges and universities are normally categorized into five classes: doctorate-granting research universities, comprehensive universities usually having graduate programs, liberal arts colleges mostly for undergraduates, community colleges, and specialized institutions providing particular professional training. No classification scheme covers every nuance of the 3,587 accredited colleges and universities in the United States, let alone the estimated 1,000 unaccredited institutions and 8,469 other vocational outlets, but a new type of institution is emerging that fits, however awkwardly, into all five of the principal categories ("The Nation," 1989). In fact, it combines core elements of all five.

One to three dozen established institutions, if opinion prevails over definition, can be identified in this new, all-purpose category. The numbers are very likely to grow. Economic and political pressures could well make this model a major trend for American higher education in the 1990s. It has already generated national and international attention.

"Partnership universities" appears to be the most appropriate label because it conveys how these institutions express themselves externally. Alternative appellations include "community universities," "cooperative or alliance universities," "interactive universities," and "corporate universities." Nomenclature debates in higher education are of marginal significance, but, for the record, the word "community" seems less appropriate because institutional externalities are not just local, and the word "interactive" presents a problem since all institutions are interactive in some measure, hence the label is just too broad. "Corporate universities," an idea with Japanese and American roots, connotes a model too hierarchial for most academic entities. Other suggested labels include "metropolitan" and "high tech."

19

## Innovative and Distinctive Features of Partnership Universities

The defining characteristics of partnership universities include both those that are essential and those that are prevalent but nonessential. Essential elements are borrowed from all five traditional institutional categories: (1) from doctorate-granting research universities, academic strength and research; applied research is more acceptable in a partnership university setting; (2) from comprehensive universities, breadth in academic offerings; in terms of size, partnership universities and colleges tend to be among the top 25 percent of American institutions of higher learning; (3) from liberal arts colleges, a core undergraduate curriculum and a balance between teaching and research; the "publish or perish" syndrome is de-emphasized and good teaching is more widely recognized; (4) from community colleges, a strong emphasis on service to the economic and cultural base of the region where the institution is located; there is a willingness to accommodate local educational and research requirements within the bounds of academic quality and integrity; and (5) from specialized institutions, the development of an academic theme or special emphasis such as computer science, specialized engineering, and public policy; the organizing theme reflects, again, the economic and cultural base of the institution's regional locale.

In the twentieth century, American higher education has been the world's most prolific incubator of new institutional formats. The partnership university is the latest manifestation of that talent. Undoubtedly, this new model will serve as the basis for still further institutional changes. During the 1980s, delegations from Europe, Japan, China, and the Soviet Union, among others, traveled to the United States to familiarize themselves with these institutional developments.

The message that these foreign visitors have taken home translates to two features of partnership universities: external responsiveness and partnership cooperation. First, these universities are responsive to their external environments and eschew the institutional isolation found frequently at other colleges and universities. Although the stereotype of academic arrogance derives from a retreat from external involvement, distance from society's day-to-day vicissitudes—Sainte-Beuve's 1869 coinage of the phrase "ivory tower" describes well the arrogant isolation—is part of a university's societal role, and it has served the academy well. Partnership universities keep their distance too in the sense that they are not slaves to the whims of their geographical regions. But their orientation, nonetheless, is avowedly toward serving the social needs of their locales, limited only by those academic and operational values requisite to any high-quality academic setting.

The regional social services rendered by a partnership university are not necessarily part of some master design or altruistic purpose. Advocates of strategic planning, for example, underscore the importance of "monitoring" a university's external environment, but emphasis remains on maintenance of stability in a college or university's internal environment by adjusting to external conditions. With the partnership university, that attitude changes: if the region where the institution is located prospers economically, culturally, and intellectually, the college or university almost certainly will be a major beneficiary, and the institution would be wise to do what it can to help develop as much regional strength as possible. It is a variation of the "tide raises all ships" theme. These institutions will engender genuine interest in their regions, even if the bulk of their resources come from elsewhere in the form of tuition, state subsidies, or endowment income, but the degree of regional affiliation will depend principally on the attitude of each university community and its president.

## The Regional Commitment of University Leadership and Resources

At partnership universities, regional economic and cultural development is a fourth institutional function after teaching, research, and service. This means that the university's leadership is publicly visible on behalf of economic and cultural development, such as by serving on citizen boards, putting together economic development mechanisms, offering help to regional business leaders to attract new jobs to the area, and encouraging the visual and performing arts. The partnership university has thus become a prominent leader for regional dynamism and development.

Probably the two most important catalysts of this shift in orientation involve the university's leadership. In meetings with area business and cultural leaders, the university president listens to their problems and discusses ways that the university can assist in finding solutions. Willingness to listen is the key. Also, the president continually reminds his or her subordinates to be responsive to regional needs when the listening ends and the programmatic initiatives begin. Institutions too often announce grand community initiatives that over time show few results. The kind of quiet diplomacy needed, both inside the institution and in interactions between the university and the community, is missing all to often.

Regional economic and cultural development requires a significant institutional commitment in words and deeds, but the inclusion of such development among a university's principal functions does not always inspire institutionwide support. Professors and deans accustomed to the traditions of the American "ivory tower" model, prevalent over the past fifty years, can well be critical, although dissent at partnership institutions appears to dissipate once the success of the design becomes apparent. The partnership university does require a spirit of entrepreneurship, though that presents less of a problem than the traditional academic construct suggests. Entrepreneurial strains run deep in American academic culture, even if the traditional model rarely acknowledges them. American professors are likely the world's most entrepreneurial.

Also, involvement in economic and cultural development does not necessarily require a large new commitment of a university's financial resources. Partnership universities actually infuse an external orientation into their ongoing programs rather than formulate and fund separate, large-scale community service programs. In fact, as opposed to depleting resources, partnership universities can financially benefit symbiotically as the economic welfare of their home regions improves, whether from university initiatives or from those of other regional leaders. The external orientation, in short, represents a change in university culture rather than some new, vast commitment of resources.

## The Mutual Benefits of Community-University Partnerships

The key to the success of any partnership is mutual self-interest. Typically, universities and colleges extend their hands asking for gifts, and the record stands as proof that the public has been generous in response. Partnership universities also engage in such traditional "institutional advancement." Yet, true partnerships flow back and forth and both sides can tout tangible benefits; this represents the essential distinction between traditional and partnership universities.

Here are ten quick examples from the experiences of partnership institutions. In partnership with a real estate developer, utilities or roads can be built through university property, adding to the institution's asset base. In partnership with an area corporation needing help with the application of some advanced technology, new professorships can be supported or special seminars can be convened. In partnership with an area hospital, a clinic can be established to help indigent clients and provide training opportunities for students. In partnership with a government agency, a joint program can be established to involve other universities and corporations in data-base development or applied research programs. In partnership with building contractors and land developers, student housing, lease-back facilities, and research parks and facilities can be developed on university land. In partnership with area cultural organizations, university facilities can be constructed to make the university more of a community cultural center. In partnership with regional community colleges, articulation agreements, joint programs, and computer registration networks can be developed—in traditional university consortia, two-year institutions and others not in the "class" of the local senior university are too frequently excluded. In partnership with some regional economic development authority, self-funding courses and programs can be offered that are attractive to a company considering relocation to the area. In partnership with public or private agencies, the university can act as a foundation to fund a consortia of universities or research institutes or to perform other services that an agency would have trouble accomplishing by itself. And in partnership with other regional leaders, the university president can become a high-profile advocate for economic and cultural development, including contacts with companies that are considering local investments. The nature of the partnerships will, by definition, vary by location, but mutual self-interest is the common denominator.

Partnership universities are assisted, almost always, by an advisory council of regional leaders. Most American colleges and universities have such advisory groups, but usually they are designed for "talking to" by academicians rather than "listening to" external constituencies. Frequently, fund-raising is the sole overt or covert purpose. At partnership universities, in contrast, advisory council members provide advice that is taken seriously by the academics. Ideally, council members divide into task forces to find ways of working on problems of mutual interest to the community and university, where the topics are chosen by the members themselves. Skillful university leaders guide the advisory council's work so that conflicts of interest are avoided.

In fact, traditional academic values of independence and freedom need not suffer in the partnership arrangement. Most advisory councils and external interests are sensitive to the need for academic integrity. And even if that sensitivity fails, partnership universities can opt to ignore the advice offered. So too, new programs will not work if university officials cannot persuade faculty and staff to incorporate them into ongoing work or, more likely, if the appropriate faculty members and staff are not involved at the outset. In short, there exist many safeguards to academic ethics and practice, reinforced in practical terms by common sense and gentle persuasion by university officials. Partnership universities demonstrate that regional involvements can bring beneficial results to the university communities in the form of greater resources, consultation opportunities, summer research projects, and the like.

## Common Traits and Thematic Variations

In addition to the two principal characteristics of commitment to an external orientation and the building of extensive community alliances, partnership universities around the United States exhibit other similarities. Given the breadth of American higher education, exceptions exist, but the public partnership institutions are generally more salient than the private ones, presumably because they are under greater pressure to perform a public service. Also, they are more likely to be located in urban or suburban settings, simply because more partnership opportunities exist in metropolitan areas.

Further, the institutions themselves are more likely to be comprehensive in scale, with 5,000 students or more; they need to have breadth to mount adequate responses to external opportunities. These institutions almost always feature graduate programs and adult students. Successful partnership universities are also less likely to adhere to traditional academic totems. Finally, these universities are likely to have leadership structures that take risks. Without such innovative leadership, especially from the university president, there is no way for the partnership format to succeed.

As these partnership universities have evolved—George Mason University, the University of Houston at Clear Lake, the University of Central Florida, Miami-Dade Community College District, the University of California at Irvine, and the University of Texas at Dallas are examples—they typically have developed themes or strengths for which they are particularly well known in their respective areas. For example, at George Mason, the theme is information science; at Irvine, it is biotechnology; at Clear Lake, it is space science; at Dallas, it is electronics. These themes reflect the regional environments and serve as bases for developing national academic standing. Many universities can lay claim to elements inherent to partnerships, but the number that incorporate most or all of the characteristics is still relatively small.

Partnership universities mark a further evolutionary step in American higher education. They are at one and the same time responsive to national and to local needs. They are very contemporary in outlook, but they have not abandoned traditional scholarly values. The partnership university model merits careful examination by any college or university that purports to be concerned about issues of regional and national concern. The model is, on the whole, a viable institutional strategy for initiation and maintenance of economic and cultural development.

## Reference

"The Nation." *Chronicle of Higher Education Almanac*, September 6, 1989, p. 5.

*Thomas M. Stauffer is president and professor of public policy at the University of Houston–Clear Lake in Houston, Texas.*

*The turbulent environment projected for many colleges and*
*universities in the 1990s will require well-oriented, educated, and*
*active governing boards.*

# The 1990s: The Decade of Trustees

*Richard P. Chait*

Clark Kerr recently observed that the 1960s were the decade of students, the 1970s the decade of faculty, the 1980s the decade of management, and the 1990s will be the decade of trustees. Kerr's prediction for the 1990s seems plausible enough. A number of ongoing trends are likely to accelerate and thereby heighten the prominence and influence of governing boards. Among these trends are (1) federal and state regulations and court decisions that underscore the authority *and* liability of governing boards and thus prompt trustees to become better informed, more involved, and increasingly vigilant; (2) intensified calls for accountability that promote "business-like behaviors" such as marketing, strategic planning, and performance appraisal, areas where trustees have considerable expertise; and (3) mounting public resistance to the spiraling price of higher education that places pressure on boards to cure the so-called cost disease.

The exponentially increasing needs of the institutions elevate the importance of the boards as sources of money, whether acquired through personal giving or through access to public and private funds. Moreover, growing expectations for colleges and universities to function as engines of the economy—training a competitive work force and conducting research that creates new products and new jobs—strengthens ties between the campuses and corporations, with trustees serving as crucial intermediaries. Finally, the precarious position of the college president, under pressure to meet the expectations of a growing number of constituencies, fosters a greater dependence on the board for counsel and support.

Thus, boards appear destined to play an increasingly significant role in campus life during the 1990s. Whether that proves to be for better or for worse depends in no small part on how effectively presidents and other senior administrators work with their respective boards (Herman, 1989). Some presidents, either supremely self-confident or skeptical of the board's abilities to make sound decisions, adopt a strategy of damage control, designed to ensure that the boards inflict minimal or no harm. Favorite tactics include attempts to divert the boards' attention from crucial to trivial matters and to bury the boards beneath mountains of unimportant information (Chait and Taylor, 1989). In the decade ahead, this treatment of trustees as little more than a necessary appendage may be especially unwise. Since boards are likely to play a pivotal role in the 1990s, presidents (and indeed campus communities) would be better advised to strengthen the boards' performance. Make no mistake, however, board development is hard work and it cannot be accomplished by the president alone. Nonetheless, the president bears a primary responsibility.

Over the course of the past three years, Holland, Chait, and Taylor (1989) interviewed over 120 trustees and presidents at twenty-two independent liberal arts colleges and universities. From these data, my colleagues and I constructed a set of six board competencies that are associated with effective trusteeship and, not incidentally, with positive financial and academic institutional performance. Also, the site visits and data analysis revealed some steps presidents can take to help improve board performance. If Kerr's prediction proves to be correct, then any measures that enhance a board's effectiveness will rank among the most useful actions a president can initiate in order to meet the challenges of the 1990s.

### Trustee Orientation

Imagine that a college president has been appointed to the board of directors of Goodyear Tire and Rubber Company. The president receives copies of the company's latest annual report, financial audit, and statement of director responsibilities. The CEO arranges a day-long visit to Akron, Ohio, which includes a tour of corporate headquarters and a nearby manufacturing plant, a series of half-hour meetings with senior managers, and an introductory conversation with union leaders. How well prepared is this president, who has kicked some tires in his day, to serve on Goodyear's board?

Too often the orientation programs for university and college trustees are not much more useful than the above, hypothetical example of a college president joining a company's board of directors: a newcomer receives a copy of the catalog, the auditor's report, and the board bylaws, a tour of the campus, and conversations with senior staff, faculty, and student leaders. Presumably, then, this corporate officer is now ready to serve as a trustee.

Some very important ingredients are missing. To be effective, new board members need to understand the institutional context, including an

orientation to the academic profession generally and to local values, traditions, and norms more specifically. In other words, trustees need to understand both the industry and the business of academia.

To better appreciate the local context, new (and not so new) trustees
should be exposed to the institution's history, lore, and hallmark characteristics. Trustees need to understand the "corporate culture," the heuristics,
and the unwritten rules. Some of this information might be communicated
effectively by tribal elders such as senior faculty and trustee emeriti. Other
aspects can be conveyed by current staff, trustees, and students and through
pamphlets designed expressly for the purpose of educating trustees.

As much as colleges recognize the importance of initiation rites for
freshmen, often setting aside an entire week for the process, these same
institutions too frequently deprive trustees of an equally necessary and
equally valuable orientation. If a board bears responsibility for a college's
future, then trustees must understand the institution's past. If a board is to
safeguard a college's values, then trustees need to know well what the
institution stands for in the first place.

## Trustee Education

Some lawyers die intestate and many shoemakers' shoes go unsoled. Similarly, many colleges do little to educate trustees even though teaching is
their principal mission.

Effective boards are composed of learners, individuals eager for information. Holland, Chait, and Taylor (1989) observed numerous instances
where effective boards set aside several hours a day, or even more, to
become better informed on substantive issues of immediate or long-term
concern to the colleges or universities served. Among the topics studied
were fund accounting, general education, academic tenure, admissions criteria, student demographics, and the political economy of South Africa.
Many boards reserve one meeting a year exclusively for educational purposes, that is, to learn and talk about a crucial issue facing their particular
institutions or higher education more broadly. Other boards periodically
discuss essays, articles, or excerpts from books that address a salient issue.
Educational activities among effective boards extend to matters of process
as well as substance. Thus, some retreats are organized around topics such
as board composition, self-study, or communication with key constituencies.

Invariably, the president plays a lead role: first, by modeling the behavior as the institution's "number one learner"; second, by encouraging board
members to raise questions and seek information; and third, by suggesting
topics of discussion to the board and facilitating their learning. The multiple payoffs of trustee education were aptly summarized by one president,
an interviewee, who organized an afternoon discussion session around
sabbatical leaves and the requirement that faculty return for at least one

year after a sabbatical: "The point is that the board really learned a lot about what the policy-making process is all about, how they go about facing difficult problems and examining all sides of them in order to work out conclusions that allow everyone to retain some parts of what they believe to be important and to move ahead effectively."

## Group Development

Among the colleges we visited with effective boards, the president and the trustees were attentive to a fundamental, yet often overlooked, facet of trusteeship: a governing board is a *group* (Alderfer, 1986). Effective boards are more akin to an orchestra than a jazz band, or more like the Los Angeles Lakers than a collection of all-star basketball players.

Presidents associated with effective boards helped cultivate a sense of cohesiveness and a sensitivity to the board's *collective* welfare in several ways. First, and most directly, the presidents had worked assiduously to create opportunities for board members to interact informally in diverse settings and roles. Thus, as one president reported, "My wife and I started having all of the board members and their spouses to dinner, trying to get these folks to know one another outside their formal roles. I've tried to get to know each one personally, to find out about their interests, their strengths, and ways they can take on tasks that really interest and involve them." As presidents enable trustees to know one another as fellow lovers of art, music, cuisine, and the like, board members can accumulate "social credits" with each other. With broadly based relationships trustees are less likely to question each other's motives (as opposed to reasons) when differences of opinion arise.

Second, presidents of colleges or universities with effective boards encourage the boards to establish group goals closely linked to, yet distinct from, overall institutional aims. The most common goal involves a commitment by each board member to contribute or raise a specified sum toward a capital campaign or annual fund. In other cases, presidents have prompted boards to adopt (sometimes publicly) goals that concern, for example, improved communication with faculty and students, more systematic self-scrutiny, or revision of the board's bylaws. As one president commented with reference to the successful completion of a board development effort, "We made our goal, built our building, and, more important, the trustees believe in themselves."

Finally, presidents associated with effective boards foster group development by ensuring that all trustees have equal access to information. This inclusive approach to sharing information helps to avoid the "nobody ever tells me anything" syndrome, which can so easily undermine a group's esprit de corps. One of the presidents interviewed sends a monthly newsletter to board members so that the out-of-towners are not uninformed about activities more readily known to local trustees. A president might even go so far as to ask trustees to write down and submit anonymously at the end of each meeting questions about "everything you've always wanted to know about the college but were afraid to ask." These queries could then be answered in a presidential memorandum or at the next board meeting.

## Campus Governance

Presidents on campuses with effective boards created and fostered multiple channels of communication between trustees and members of key constituencies. These structures included open forums with trustees, joint task forces, committees composed of students, faculty, and board members, lunches and dinners, and annual reports by the board to the campus community. At one college the president even invited several dissident faculty members to a board retreat to participate in the process of setting priorities for an upcoming development campaign. The same president encouraged a campus forum on divestment, with a board member and the student council president as co-chairs.

These astute presidents realized that trustees must have opportunities—some formal, some informal, but all coordinated through the president's office—for personal contact with members of the campus community. Such engagements help debunk the misguided and occasionally venal stereotypes that some trustees hold about faculty and students, and vice versa. And perhaps most important, discussions between the board and campus groups often lead to better ideas and to consensus about how to improve the institution.

## Strategic Direction

In the course of our site visits, we observed that presidents on campuses with effective boards regularly placed issues before the boards within the larger context of the institutions' missions and strategies.

There are several procedures presidents can employ to focus board attention on strategic questions. A three- to five-page annual statement of strategy by the presidents provides a useful touchstone and springboard. This memorandum outlines the president's vision for the college and the principal means to achieve the stated objectives. Then, whenever the president presents an issue for the board's consideration, he or she can provide an introductory statement, orally or in writing, that explicitly explains *why* the matter is before the board and *how* the item relates to the institution's mission and strategy.

Colleges and universities have now had enough experience with strategic planning to appreciate that both mission and strategy must be responsive to the powerful influences exerted by the external environment. The

1990s promise to be no less turbulent than the 1980s in regard to demographic, financial, legal, political, and technical developments. Uniquely situated at the boundaries of the campus and the larger society, trustees are particularly well suited to scan the environment and consider the implications for the campus. Therefore, a president eager to maximize the board's contributions will encourage trustees to focus on the relationships between the larger environment and the institution's long-term welfare. In one case, such effort included a presentation to the board by a futurist for a multinational oil company. In another instance, the board had a day-long discussion of the president's vision for the college in 1994 and the possible impact of various external forces. In each case, the president proposed and shaped the agenda and capitalized on the board's desire and ability to address questions of strategic direction.

## Conclusion

There seems to be little doubt that the 1990s will present a turbulent environment for most colleges and universities. Competition for resources—students, dollars, faculty, and equipment—will be keen and often unpredictable. In this environment, boards of trustees are among the steadier, more predictable resources that can be nourished to cope with the challenges that lie ahead.

For the reasons noted at the outset of this chapter, most colleges and universities in the decade ahead will probably have greater and more frequent need for effective boards. Whether the boards in fact respond effectively depends to a considerable degree on whether they have been well oriented, educated, and nurtured and on whether they play an integral role in their respective campus communities and organizational strategies. These conditions, in turn, depend to a large degree on the campus presidents. As reported here, our study of effective boards revealed some practical, concrete steps presidents can take toward that end.

## References

Alderfer, C. "The Invisible Director on Corporate Boards." *Harvard Business Review,* 1986, *64* (6), 38–52.

Chait, R. P., and Taylor, B. E. "Charting the Territory of Nonprofit Boards." *Harvard Business Review,* 1989, *67* (1), 44–54.

Herman, R. D. "Board Functions and Board-Staff Relations in Non-Profit Organizations: An Introduction." In R. Herman and J. Van Til (eds.), *Non-Profit Boards of Directors: Analyses and Applications.* New Brunswick, N.J.: Transaction, 1989.

Holland, T. P., Chait, R. P., and Taylor, B. E. *Institutional Governance: Identifying and Measuring Board Competencies.* College Park, Md.: National Center for Postsecondary Governance and Finance, 1989.

*Richard P. Chait is professor of higher education and management, and executive director, National Center for Postsecondary Governance and Finance, University of Maryland, College Park.*

*A rapidly changing academic marketplace will transform the faculty and shape critical aspects of the faculty's role during the 1990s.*

# Faculty Issues in the 1990s: New Realities, New Opportunities

*Jack H. Schuster*

Speculating about the faculty of the future is not without hazards. Nonetheless, the faculty of the 1990s is largely in place, and an outline of most of the issues of likely salience is now visible as the new decade unfolds.

It is axiomatic that the overall effectiveness of higher education in the 1990s will be intimately and inextricably linked to the faculty of the 1990s, that is, to the faculty's quality and commitment. The central point is that a college or university—large or small, public or independent, two-year or four-year—cannot conceivably accomplish its basic missions without a faculty adequate in size, quality, and commitment. While some observers may take issue with an assertion that the faculty *is* the university, it would be difficult to quarrel with the proposition that faculty performance is the most influential factor bearing on an institution's efforts to fulfill its teaching, research, and public service missions. This point has been stated concisely by Komisar (1983, p. 9): "All that is accomplished by the Academy is a product of the competence, enthusiasm, and energy of its faculty."

My main thesis is that the 1990s will be a period of major change for the faculty, and this change in turn has far-reaching implications for higher education. I thus focus here on the kinds of changes that will most affect faculty, hence higher education, in the coming decade.

## An Unkind Era

As a point of departure, the following list summarizes succinctly the context in which faculty members have been working over the past two decades, and in which they have experienced numerous unpleasantries:

 33

• The real income of faculty declined sharply. From the historic high reached in 1972-1973, real income plummeted over the next eight years. Then, over the following eight-year period (from 1981-1982 through 1988-1989), faculty salaries rebounded as increases averaged 1.7 percent per year above the Consumer Price Index (American Association of University Professors, 1990). This rebound amounts to a partial recovery, but the cumulative loss in real earnings for faculty since the early 1970s appears to be greater than that for any other major, nonagricultural occupation.

• The faculty's voice in campus governance has been diluted as the locus of decision making has shifted toward management-minded administrations and various entities, governmental and otherwise, situated beyond the campus boundaries (Schuster, Miller, and Associates, 1989).

• The ranks of faculty members have been swollen by the infusion of scores of thousands of part-time faculty who, while bringing talent and commitment to their tasks, have changed the composition of "the faculty" and have altered what it means to be a faculty member on any given campus.

• The status of faculty members has declined. For higher education in general, the decade of the 1970s began with turbulent protests against the war in Southeast Asia. In some respects, faculty credibility was battered in that process, and, along with many other institutions and professions in our society, the prior level of occupational esteem has not been fully recovered.

• Most faculty members have found themselves stuck, their aspirations often blunted. That is, in striking contrast to the late 1950s and 1960s, most faculty, since then, have been trapped in a stagnant labor market.

• As a consequence of the foregoing developments (among others), faculty morale, by most accounts, has been uneven, dropping to very low levels on many campuses.

Although these developments are troubling, faculty lives have not been miserable. For some, misery may be an apt description, and for many—perhaps a majority—the quality of academic life surely has declined during this twenty-year period. But most faculty members still enjoy what they do and frequently even love what they do. Whatever the decibel level of complaints, very few faculty members, in all but a few fields, have opted to abandon academic careers.

Looking ahead now, the 1990s are likely to bring extraordinary changes—even some convulsions—for a faculty that has been mired for two decades in relatively inhospitable circumstances, changes that will shape and, at least to some degree, transform higher education. Much of what I foresee derives from my assessment of a dramatically changing academic labor market.

## The Academic Labor Market in the 1990s

Vectors of supply and demand exert powerful influences on academic life. Both supply and demand, although especially the latter, will change so significantly in the next decade that the consequences for faculty will be profound.

**Demand.** The academic marketplace now stands at the brink of upheaval. Within a handful of years, certainly before the end of the decade, the labor market for academics will undergo a substantial and dramatic transformation. Current demographic data foretell the developments. Fueled by expanding enrollments in higher education (as the offspring of the so-called baby boomers begin to matriculate) and by unprecedented numbers of faculty vacancies (as legions of aging faculty retire), the marketplace of academe, relatively stagnant for nearly two decades, is destined to vibrate with activity.

A few specific projections help to dramatize the contention that demand will mushroom: (1) The seven-campus Minnesota State University System (1989, p. 1) has estimated that it will need to replace 70 percent of its faculty over the next fifteen years. (2) At Columbia University, "nearly half of the tenured professors in the arts and sciences will retire in the 1990s" (Sovern, 1989, p. 6). (3) The California Postsecondary Education Commission (1988, p. 27), drawing on studies by each of the three public higher education segments, has estimated that "the public postsecondary systems will be replacing approximately 64 percent of their current faculty within the next 12 years" (that is, by the year 2000). This adds up to approximately 24,000 new hires, not including the independent sector. (4) A recent study concluded that "the next 15 years will witness a steep increase in the annual net loss of college faculty, the replacement of whom may be exacerbated by growth in the overall size of the professoriate" (McGuire and Price, 1989, p. 7; see Mooney, 1989a). Drawing on a sample of twenty-nine campuses (twenty-five of them liberal arts colleges), the authors estimated that "the annual replacement need [for faculty] in the year 2003 is projected to be 37% higher than it was in 1989." This list could be expanded substantially as studies of this kind continue to point in the direction of sharply escalating demand.

The most recent major study of the academic labor market (Bowen and Sosa 1989) focuses on demand and supply for doctorate-holding faculty in the arts and sciences at four-year institutions. The subset of faculty they studied, numbering 139,350 in 1987 (p. 28), constitutes roughly one-third of all full-time faculty at postsecondary institutions.

Paying considerable attention to disaggregated data, that is, to demand data broken down by various arts and sciences fields, the authors project that more than half of the faculty (74,144 or 53.2 percent) will have departed by the year 2002. Projecting to 2012, the authors estimate that the total demand for new arts and sciences doctorates at four-year institutions, stemming both from replacements and net new positions, will range between 150,496 and 181,314 (p. 126). In all, this study provides further evidence of substantial faculty turnover in the proximate future.

Similarly, Bowen and Schuster (1986) provide a forecast of large numbers of new hires. Based on our projected demand data for the 1990s, I estimate that American colleges and universities will need to make on the order of 180,000 appointments just in this new decade, with most of these vacancies occurring in the second half of the decade. Moreover, the bulk of anticipated retirements will come *after* 1999, and, using the same methodology, we anticipate the necessity of making an additional 160,000 or so appointments between the years 2000 and 2004. Thus, over the next fifteen years, we foresee the need to find roughly 340,000 new faculty members. Considering that the total full-time faculty today totals approximately 465,000, these projected numbers of new faculty are sobering.

**Supply.** The less predictable part of the labor market equation involves estimates of supply. For example, although supply will certainly follow demand to some degree, just how greatly supply of new faculty from traditional sources (that is, graduate schools) will expand is difficult to forecast (see the discussion of market "adjustment mechanisms" in Bowen and Sosa, 1989, pp. 144–171). Also, there are many pools of potential supply, such as part-time faculty and those persons who never gained entree to faculty positions. Their attractiveness to employing colleges has not yet been fully tested. In addition, there is the important question of whether the more marginal liberal arts colleges and the comprehensive colleges and universities will find holders of master's degrees to be acceptable when individuals with doctorates are in short supply. These significant uncertainties aside, the overarching question is whether or not an adequate number of suitably qualified men and women will be available to fill the impending vacancies. In answer, there is little basis for optimism, for essentially three reasons:

First, for more than a decade a relatively smaller proportion of the most able undergraduates has been attracted to Ph.D. programs and hence drawn into academic careers than was previously the case. Put another way, the competitors for the most talented minds, namely, professional schools and more lucrative careers (particularly in business and law), have enjoyed impressive success when pitted against graduate schools. It is not surprising, of course, that academe fares poorly in the competition during an era when relatively few job openings in higher education exist. And even though the academy *may* now be regaining its allure vis-a-vis the competition, the comparative unattractiveness of academic careers has been a reality, not just conjecture, throughout much of the 1970s and 1980s.

Second, it takes a while to produce doctorate holders. On average, approximately 10.5 years elapse between receiving a baccalaureate and a doctorate (National Research Council, 1989). Of course, there is considerable variation by field, and the time to degree will undoubtedly shrink as the number of available jobs expands. Nonetheless, the most perplexing faculty-related problem of the 1990s—how to find those scores of thousands of new faculty members—is upon us *now*, and there is virtually no way that adequate numbers of suitably qualified prospective faculty members will be available prior to the end of this decade.

Third, despite the emphasis in this analysis on quantity, the point must be underscored that the problem is not exclusively, or even primarily, a matter of numbers. As Howard Bowen has observed over the years, history demonstrates that, allowing for exceptions in a few fields, there will be a sufficient number of individuals eager to step forward to claim academic jobs (Bowen and Schuster, 1986, p. 169). The crucial question though, concerns *quality*, that is, just how qualified will those people be? The answer is a cause for deep concern.

There is already evidence that it is getting tougher to find and hire qualified faculty. One indicator is found in El-Khawas (1989, pp. 2, 18–19), based on a survey of 366 campuses by the American Council on Education. Among the most significant findings are that faculty shortages already exist in some high-demand fields, "half of all colleges and universities reported it now takes them longer to find qualified persons for full-time faculty positions," and "there is greater difficulty in getting top applicants to accept faculty positions offered them" (p. 2).

Moreover, a recent national survey of faculty members (National Survey of Postsecondary Faculty), conducted by the NCES (National Center for Education Statistics, 1990) in conjunction with SRI International and the Center for the Study of Higher Education at Pennsylvania State University, provides more unsettling news: sizable proportions of faculty members indicated that they would consider leaving their institutions, and higher education altogether, if the right opportunity appeared. Such talk may be "cheap," for over the years faculty, even in the most difficult of times, have abandoned academic careers only in very small proportions. Even so, the NCES survey reveals an undercurrent of dissatisfaction with prevailing conditions in academe.

So, there is mounting evidence that the marketplace has already begun to shift. When the shortages of qualified faculty members really become acute, toward the end of the decade, a much different recruitment dynamic will prevail. Competition will become intense. Institution raiding on a fairly large scale, especially for scarce minority faculty, is inevitable. Indeed, Mooney (1989b, p. 1) proclaims that "a recruiting frenzy" has already taken hold to lure minority faculty. The result will be that institutions currently rich in faculty are destined to get richer—or, at a minimum hold their own—while the poor are going to have to scramble mightily just to field a minimally qualified faculty by decade's end. Michael Sovern (1989, p. 17), president of Columbia University, has sounded an anxious note in speaking about the probable consequences of demand for faculty outstripping supply:

> As more faculty vacancies occur, and competition for the most talented graduate students intensifies, relatively few universities will be able to replenish their academic strength. The fate of the remainder—the majority of America's institutions of higher learning, including many important universities—is in doubt. If they are forced to grant tenure to the second-rate, the downward spiral could become irreversible. Many institutions will have little choice: even as the supply of talent dwindles, the demand for college teachers will boom.

## Beyond the Marketplace

While conditions that affect faculty, other than the labor market itself, are not likely to change rapidly, the 1990s afford the prospect of a number of significant, related changes, many of which will enhance the professional lives of faculty members. Consider the evolution of professional development. Faculty development has probably existed as long as there have been faculty members. But it was not until the 1960s that a faculty development movement crystallized, spawning specialists and programs that focused on the improvement of instructional skills. Hundreds of campus programs sprang up, and in many instances their scope broadened over time to encompass other aspects of professional development. Since the mid-1980s, that attention has been directed in a systematic way to the *personal* dimension of faculty development.

The 1990s are likely to be a time of increasing emphasis on the personal dimension of faculty development. This prediction is based on two facts. One, the age distribution of faculty will be shifting to a new and unprecedented configuration as, at one end of the age continuum, a large cohort of faculty members nears retirement while, at the other end, unprecedented numbers of young neophytes enter academic careers. This skewed distribution defines a *bimodal* faculty, that is, a faculty overrepresented, by historical norms, in the most senior *and* the most junior ranks and correspondingly underrepresented in the middle rank of faculty in their forties to mid-fifties.

This imbalance in the faculty presents a formidable challenge: the formulation of campus-based programs specially targeted to meet the needs of both the young, relatively inexperienced faculty and the most senior faculty members. On this front, much work remains to be done (Schuster, Wheeler, and Associates, 1990).

Other issues that likely will shape faculty well-being and performance in the 1990s include the following:

- *The tension between research and teaching:* What can be done to bring into closer harmony the commonly perceived, competing objectives of teaching and research? Can the faculty reward system be modified to respond more effectively to faculty members' individual preferences for emphasizing one or the other? Will emerging, broader conceptions of scholarship influence what institutions expect of their faculty members and afford those faculty greater latitude in setting their own priorities?

- *Race and gender equity:* What can be done to attract to academic careers (and to retain) persons from already severely underrepresented groups of racial minorities? And, similarly, what can be done to attract and retain women—especially in those fields in which they are extremely underrepresented?

- *Undercompensation:* Will it be possible for faculty members, in a decade in which resources undoubtedly will remain scarce, to make up the economic ground lost in the 1970s and only partially recovered in the 1980s? The projected scarcity of qualified faculty members should translate into higher levels of compensation, but will it?

- *The faculty role in governance:* Will faculty members find ways in the 1990s to become more effectively involved in governance processes? Amid the pressures of academic life, will a sufficient number of faculty members be drawn to the difficult, time-consuming business of governance?

## An Agenda for Institutions

What can colleges and universities now begin to do about resolving these faculty issues? Here, briefly, are several ideas that warrant consideration.

1. One crucial need is to facilitate data gathering and analyses on a range of topics. These topics include anticipated faculty retirements, anticipated postsecondary enrollments, and, consequently, estimates of the quantity and quality of foreseeable new hires.

2. It is very important to recover the lost art of encouraging highly able undergraduates, especially at the junior-year level, to consider academic careers. Such programs are not difficult to organize and need not be costly. Indeed, faculty members appear to be more willing now than in recent years to advise students that this is an opportune time to pursue an academic career (Carnegie Foundation for the Advancement of Teaching, 1989, pp. 73, 88).

3. There is an urgent need to take special account of the existing underrepresentation of minorities among campus faculties. It is a virtual certainty that the underrepresentation, especially of blacks and Hispanics, will become progressively more acute unless dramatic interventions are launched, identifying talented prospective faculty and providing substantial support—tangible and psychological—aimed at making attractive the choice of an academic career.

## Conclusion

In the 1990s, the composition of faculties will begin to metamorphose as scores of thousands of professors retire and are replaced by predominantly younger men and women. Because faculty members in many instances will be in scarcer supply than has been the case for two decades, a different dynamic of campus relationships, based on that emerging social demand, *may* arise. Will faculty members—for the most part unaccustomed to institutional courting—find that their new situation gives them more leverage? More bargaining power regarding compensation and research support? More influence over the mix of their responsibilities? Will these faculty come to resemble the students of the past two decades of "student consumerism"—that is, in short supply and hence beneficiaries of intensified campus policies to recruit and retain them?

There is, too, the danger that the quality of higher education will suffer from a severe shortfall in qualified faculty. Although we are not able to identify with any precision the adverse consequences of an inadequately prepared faculty, those consequences could be severe, even deadly, unless we muster the savvy and commitment necessary to soften the effects. Thus, increasing the supply of qualified faculty constitutes one of the most formidable tasks that will confront faculty, administrators, and public policymakers alike in the new decade.

While it is, of course, too early to tell what will happen, the crucial fact remains that the faculty situation will become far more fluid and dynamic than has been the case in several decades. Though colleges and universities will encounter formidable challenges in the academic labor market, those institutions and their faculty members will have opportunities to transform the processes of higher education.

## References

American Association of University Professors. "Some Dynamic Aspects of Academic Careers: The Urgent Need to Match Aspirations with Compensation. The Annual Report on the Economic Status of the Profession, 1989-90." *Academe*, 1990, 76 (2), 3–29.

Bowen, H. R., and Schuster, J. H. *American Professors: A National Resource Imperiled.* New York: Oxford University Press, 1986.

Bowen, W. G., and Sosa, J. A. *Prospects for Faculty in the Arts and Sciences: A Study of Factors Affecting Demand and Supply, 1987 to 2012.* Princeton, N.J.: Princeton University Press, 1989.

California Postsecondary Education Commission. *Diversification of the Faculty and Staff in California Public Postsecondary Education from 1977 to 1987.* Report 88-29. Sacramento: California Postsecondary Education Commission, 1988.

Carnegie Foundation for the Advancement of Teaching. *The Condition of the Professoriate: Attitudes and Trends, 1989.* Princeton, N.J.: Carnegie Foundation for the Advancement of Teaching, 1989.

El-Khawas, E. *Campus Trends, 1989.* Higher Education Panel Reports, no. 78. Washington, D.C.: American Council on Education, 1989.

Komisar, J. B. "Investing in Our Faculty." Paper prepared at the Wingspread Conference on Faculty Exchange, Racine, Wis., July 25, 1983.

McGuire, M. D., and Price, J. A. "Faculty Replacement Needs for the Next 15 Years: A Simulated Attrition Model." Paper presented at the twenty-ninth annual forum of the Association for Institutional Research, May 1989.

Minnesota State University System. *Recruitment and Retention of Quality Faculty and Administrators.* Saint Paul: Minnesota State University System, 1989.

Mooney, C. J. "In 2003, Colleges May Need to Recruit a Third More Professors than in '89." *Chronicle of Higher Education,* July 19, 1989a.

Mooney, C. J. "Affirmative-Action Goals, Coupled with Tiny Numbers of Minority Ph.D.'s, Set Off Faculty Recruiting Frenzy." *Chronicle of Higher Education,* August 2, 1989b.

National Center for Education Statistics. *Faculty in Higher Education Institutions, 1988.* (1988 National Survey of Postsecondary Faculty; NCES Publication No. 90-365.) Washington, D.C.: U.S. Department of Education, Office of Educational Research and Improvement, 1990.

National Research Council. *Summary Report 1988: Doctorate Recipients for United States Universities.* Washington, D.C.: National Academy Press, 1989.

Schuster, J. H., Miller, L. H., and Associates. *Governing Tomorrow's Campus: Perspectives and Agendas.* New York: American Council on Education/Macmillan, 1989.

Schuster, J. H., Wheeler, D. W., and Associates. *Enhancing Faculty Careers: Strategies for Development and Renewal.* San Francisco: Jossey-Bass, 1990.

Sovern, M. J. "Higher Education: The Real Crisis." *Columbia: The Magazine of Columbia University,* June-July 1989. (Reprinted from the *New York Times Magazine,* January 22, 1989.)

*Jack H. Schuster is professor of education and public policy at the Claremont Graduate School, Claremont, California.*

*The 1990s will bring a major transformation in the role of faculty members, including greater diversity of assignments and greater interaction with off-campus communities.*

# Expectations of and by Faculty: An Overview for the 1990s

*Frederic Jacobs*

It has become commonplace to describe as "enormous" and "astonishing" the changes in American higher education since the early 1960s. At that time, colleges and universities, faced with burgeoning student populations and social and political upheaval, began to assume the characteristics that are identified with contemporary American postsecondary education: administrative and programmatic complexity; heterogeneity of purpose and audience; expansion of programs, missions, and student constituencies; fiscal constraints despite rapidly increasing tuition and appropriation revenues; and increasing reliance on federally insured loans as well as direct aid to ensure participation by the economically disadvantaged.

Indeed, the magnitude of those changes across a quarter of a century is remarkable. There were and still remain, however, some elements of stability and continuity that in part defined the context in which the changes occurred. One such element has been the constancy of and expectations about the role of faculty. Specifically, there are two characteristics of college and university faculty that are of interest here: first, for most of the past twenty-five years, there have been relatively few changes in their actual and perceived roles and responsibilities; second, the profession is dominated by the large cohort recruited and hired in the 1960s, many of whom who will be leaving active service over the next two decades.

For a generation, college and university faculties have been unusually stable, in role and responsibility, in size, and in membership. And, despite impending departures and the increased inclusion of underrepresented groups, there has been a pervasive feeling that the faculty's role, variable as it may be from institution to institution, is known and knowable, stable

NEW DIRECTIONS FOR HIGHER EDUCATION, no. 70, Summer 1990 © Jossey-Bass Inc., Publishers and stabilizing, and, therefore, predictable to individual faculty members (and aspiring faculty members) and their institutions.

After so long a period of quiescence for one group within a system undergoing such a monumental upheaval, why should there be change now?

Among the prospective changes during the 1990s will be new expectations for individual performance, new requirements for activity and involvement, changed institutional resource allocations, and a substantially altered culture resulting from personnel turnover. In short, the faculty of higher education during the first decade of the twenty-first century will consist of different people, whose professional responsibilities will be expanded and varied from present realities, and who will work in an environment—and with resources—markedly different from what now exists. There are two factors that account for these predicted changes: changes in the demographics of the professoriat and changes in professional expectations.

## Changes in Demographics

In the period from 1960 to 1987, nationally, the instructional staff grew in size from 276,000 to 722,000, an increase of just over 162 percent. (During the same period, opening student enrollments each fall increased by 243 percent, from 3,660,000 to 12,544,000.) It is noteworthy that the greatest increase occurred from 1960 to 1970 (an increase of 198,000 in a decade) and from 1970 to 1975 (an additional increase of 154,000). Thus, in a fifteen-year period, the professoriat was augmented by 352,000 members from its 1960 base of 276,000. In contrast, estimates from the National Center for Educational Statistics project a decrease of 10,000 faculty members in the period from 1982 to 1997 (Andersen, Carter, and Malizio, 1989, pp. 71, 167).

This growth is significant because it indicates how much the professoriat has been dominated by the faculty group now in the middle and late years of their careers. Inevitably, so large a cohort skews the age composition of faculty. In 1975, for example, 53.5 percent of all male faculty members and 54.6 percent of all female faculty members were forty-one years of age or older; in 1985, that group had increased in size to 71.1 percent of men and 59.6 percent of women. This trend will continue throughout the 1990s (Andersen, Carter, and Malizio, 1989, p. 172).

Bowen and Sosa (1989) examine in detail this pattern of "bunching." They state that "age distributions have direct consequences for teaching, as well as for scholarship and for the academic leadership of departments and programs. The access that students have to faculty of various ages and perspectives undoubtedly influences their classroom experiences. More generally, the vitality of departments often depends on maintaining an age structure that permits an orderly infusion of new people and a reasonably stable sense of departmental direction" (Bowen and Sosa, 1989, p. 15).

Clearly, the need for faculty hiring in the period from 1960 to 1975 skewed age distribution patterns. Both Bowen and Sosa and Lozier and Dooris (Consortium on Financing Higher Education, 1987) focused on issues of faculty replacement and the predicted, impending shortages in many disciplines. Lozier and Dooris identified eight fields (visual and performing arts; education; architecture and environmental design; agriculture; engineering and engineering technology; language, area studies, humanities and letters; math, life sciences, physical sciences, and science technology; and communication) in which the proportion of faculty age fifty-five and older in fall 1986 was 25 percent or greater.

The most recent survey in the series conducted annually by the American Council on Education (El-Khawas, 1989) already documents current shortages of faculty in computer science, business, mathematics, and health professions: "Over the next five years, most of these shortages are expected to worsen. Five in ten institutions expect future shortages of computer science faculty, 4 in 10 expect future shortages of mathematics faculty, and 1 in 4 expect continued faculty shortages in the health professions. One in three expect future shortages in business" (El-Khawas, 1989, p. 2).

The inevitable consequence of these data and these trends is a focus on "replenishment," and indeed, special attention has been given to increasing Ph.D. production, increasing the participation of minorities and women in the professoriat, and actively recruiting potential faculty in disciplines experiencing acute shortages. Cartter's (1976) seminal work, along with the work of Breneman and Youn (1980) and Bowen and Sosa (1989), examines issues of supply and demand and of "replacement demand," and the projections deal with maintaining and increasing fluidity, especially in areas where shortages are identified. Appropriately, in that context, Bowen and Sosa identify graduate education as the principal focus for implementing change.

Their study, however, is prospective in its policy implications. For the present, we face a more pragmatic and immediate problem: a decade (or more) of transition with a large, powerful—and aging—cohort in place. Dealing with the needs of those faculty members and, simultaneously, beginning the planning process for the next generation of the professoriat are likely to increase internal conflict about core issues and values: programmatic development, incentive and reward structures, resource allocations, and academic governance.

The demographic realities of the present and future professoriat create a dramatic tension. The older group, politically powerful in their professional organizations and on their institutional campuses, are comfortable with the culture and expectations they have created. At the same time, those faculty members acknowledge that the system must be replenished.

But such recognition does not suggest or provide solutions. We face the present decade with two central problems: a very large and powerful cohort of faculty preparing to exit the profession and an acute, anticipated shortage of replacement faculty.

More attention has been focused on the second problem than on the first. But the 1990s are likely to be dominated by this duality, and we need to examine the present and anticipated expectations of the current faculty as part of the planning process for the twenty-first century. Even without the impending elimination of mandatory retirement (when the Age Discrimination in Retirement Act becomes effective for college and university faculty in January 1994), the current "bulge" will pass through the system, much as the "baby boomers" did.

## Changes in Expectations

Previous studies, most notably the excellent work of Caplow and McGee (1958), Ladd and Lipset (1975), and Bowen and Schuster (1986), have presented detailed descriptions of the values, careers, attitudes, and expectations of the professoriat. Broadly speaking, these studies focus on the career development of faculty, whereas the Cartter (1976) and Bowen and Sosa (1989) studies examine academic labor markets.

Faculty career development and the evolution of professional expectations have been the objects of numerous general and discipline-specific studies, especially during the period of expansion of the professoriat. In general, these faculty studies have examined the topics of entry into academic careers; rewards, incentives, and salaries; gender and race; workload; and tenure.

**Career Entry.** A common assumption of faculty members, identified in Caplow and McGee (1958), has been that the prestige of a job applicant's institution (and academic department) and the influence of the faculty adviser/advocate are more important in hiring than the evaluation of the applicant's actual academic performance. Additional research on the "halo" effect of the institution and the adviser has confirmed the phenomenon (Cole and Cole, 1973; Long, Allison, and McGinnis, 1979; Reskin, 1979).

Several factors, however, have weakened the halo effect. First, the pressures of affirmative action have made job searches more public and more open, substantially closing down the "old boy" networks of the past. In addition, there has been an increase in the availability of faculty members trained abroad whose institutions (and faculty mentors) are not known to prospective employers in the United States. Third, Ph.D. production has increased significantly in the last quarter-century, making insider networks and inferential judgments more problematic. Because annual production has more than tripled since 1960 (from 10,000 to more than 30,000 Ph.D.s), it is simply not possible to achieve for the current generation of academics what was achieved for their predecessors in regard to initial job placement.

**Rewards, Incentives, and Salaries.** No other variable more dramatically demonstrates the change in expectations of the professoriat than the increase in faculty salaries over the past twenty-five years. Average salaries have increased by more than 350 percent in the period from 1965–1966 ($9,816) to 1987–1988 ($37,000) (Andersen, Carter, and Malizio, 1989, p. 176).

Unlike other sectors within the education profession, such as elementary and secondary school teaching, salaries of college and university faculty have become increasingly competitive. And a rather elaborate system of salary differentials across disciplines has evolved (Hansen, 1985; Lewis and Becker, 1979).

Increasingly, a set of faculty expectations about salary has created tensions in many institutions. First, there is an assumption that annual salary increases should be equal to, or greater than, the current rate of inflation. Second, there is a related assumption that, as tuition rates increase, faculty salaries should increase proportionately. Neither of these assumptions can be implemented easily by institutions facing high fixed costs, plagued with problems of deferred maintenance, and coping with a faculty that is increasingly tenured, increasingly senior.

**Gender and Race.** There is a widespread belief that aggressive affirmative action programs have had a profound effect on the demographics of the professoriat. While some progress has been made, a truly heterogeneous faculty has not yet been realized. Women, who constituted 22.3 percent of full-time instructional faculty in 1972–1973, constituted only 23 percent in 1985–1986, after fifteen years of concerted effort to increase the proportion of female faculty members. A more hopeful sign for the future is the increase in female assistant professors (from 23.8 percent to 38 percent) during the same period (Andersen, Carter, and Malizio, 1989, p. 171).

The data on racial composition of full-time faculty are not encouraging: nonwhite women were represented by the same number in 1984 as in 1975 (7 percent), and the percentage of nonwhite men went from 5.7 percent in 1975 to 7 percent in 1984 (Andersen, Carter, and Malizio, 1989, p. 172). In its annual survey of colleges and universities, the American Council on Education reported that 80 percent of responding institutions indicated that affirmative action programs were in place to increase the number of minority faculty (El-Khawas, 1989, p. vi).

There is a clear expectation that American higher education can and should increase the number of women and minority faculty. But, a dual problem exists. First, until vacancies are created when the "bunched" cohort retires, there are insufficient resources available to hire and advance large numbers of new faculty. Second, at present, there appear to be shortages of women and minorities who are preparing for academic careers. This underrepresentation of women and minorities may become, as Bowen and Sosa (1989) suggest, a public policy issue throughout the decade.

**Workload.** The changed expectations of faculty members are also clearly demonstrated by issues of workload. There has always been variation in teaching load among and within institutions, based, in large measure, on institutional finances and on each institution's expectations for faculty research productivity. Inevitably, there have been faculty demands for reduced teaching loads to better enable faculty members to pursue their research agendas. A reduction in teaching from five courses to four courses per academic year, however productive a faculty member may be in his or her research, represents a 20 percent decrease in teaching availability. This decrease is, for some institutions, an intractable problem because the resources are not available to support such reductions, even when the institutional (and individual) aspirations for high research productivity and achievement remain constant.

Equally difficult, institutions continue to require more from faculty members in their service commitment. Collegial governance is time consuming, and the issues have become increasingly complex. Externally imposed requirements, including hazardous waste disposal, confidentiality of student and faculty records, affirmative action, due process for students, protection of human subjects, copyright and patent issues, and overall compliance with institutional regulations have become incorporated into the corpus of faculty responsibilities.

For public institutions, compliance with burgeoning state requirements has become a fact of life. For private institutions, accreditation requirements, such as assessment of learning, have become another faculty responsibility. And, for all faculty members who are engaged in sponsored research, grant preparation is a time-consuming, but essential, activity.

Many faculty believe that, despite reductions in teaching load, their workload expectations have increased significantly in the last decade.

**Tenure.** Another expectation of faculty is the durability of the tenure system. There have been no serious challenges to the tenure system in the United States, and during the past quarter-century of growth in the size of the professoriat, two axioms have emerged as fundamental to the tenure system. First, tenure has become a de facto right to continuous employment, with tenure rarely rescinded and then only for reasons of moral turpitude or mental incompetence. Second, tenure is presumed to guarantee an institutionally mandated hearing prior to its rescindment. While there is not yet any indication that the removal of mandatory requirement rules will alter the overall pattern of departure from the profession, the durability of tenure does create the potential for many faculty to remain in their positions indefinitely after January 1994.

## Implications

Overall, the enterprise of higher education can anticipate significant changes throughout the next decade, and well into the next century. Among the major changes anticipated are the following:

1. Change in the demography of students, with more adults and more minority students entering the system
2. Change in the age composition of faculty, with more young faculty replacing the age-"bunched" faculty now in active service
3. Change in financial support for higher education, with greater reliance on loan rather than grant programs
4. Increased support for research, especially in areas of technology
5. Increased involvement in educational collaboration, especially with the business community.

These changes, profound as they are likely to be, also reflect changes in values. Faculty members will be directly affected.

Overall, institutions and faculty members will have increased expectations of each other throughout the decade and into the next century. With careful planning, and attention to the issues outlined here, neither the institutions nor their faculty members need be disappointed.

## References

Andersen, C., Carter, D., and Malizio, A. *1989–90 Fact Book on Higher Education.* New York: American Council on Education/Macmillan, 1989.

Bowen, H. R., and Schuster, J. H. *American Professors: A National Resource Imperiled.* New York: Oxford University Press, 1986.

Bowen, W. G., and Sosa, J. A. *Prospects for Faculty in the Arts and Sciences: A Study of Factors Affecting Demand and Supply, 1987 to 2012.* Princeton, N.J.: Princeton University Press, 1989.

Breneman, D. W., and Youn, T.I.K. (eds.). *Academic Labor Markets and Careers.* New York: Falmer Press, 1988.

Caplow, T., and McGee, R. *The Academic Marketplace.* Garden City, N.Y.: Doubleday, 1958.

Cartter, A. M. *Ph.D.'s and the Academic Labor Market.* New York: McGraw-Hill, 1976.

Cole, J. R., and Cole, S. *Social Stratification in Science.* Chicago: University of Chicago Press, 1973.

Consortium on Financing Higher Education. *Early Retirement Programs for Faculty: A Survey of Thirty-Six Institutions.* Cambridge, Mass.: Consortium on Financing Higher Education, 1987.

El-Khawas, E. *Campus Trends, 1989.* Washington, D.C.: American Council on Education, 1989.

Hansen, W. L. "Salary Differentials Across Disciplines." *Academe: Bulletin of the American Association of University Professors,* July-August 1985, pp. 6-7.

Ladd, E. C., and Lipset, S. M. *1975 Survey of the American Professoriate*. Storrs: University of Connecticut Press, 1975.

Lewis, D. R., and Becker, W. E. (eds.). *Academic Rewards in Higher Education*. Cambridge, Mass.: Ballinger, 1979.

Long, J. S., Allison, P. D., and McGinnis, R. "Entrance into the Academic Career." *American Sociological Review*, 1979, 44, 816–830.

Reskin, B. "Academic Sponsorship and Scientist Careers." *Sociology of Education*, 1979, 52, 129–146.

*Frederic Jacobs is dean of faculties and professor of education at American University, Washington, D.C.*

*Lessons learned about strategic planning in the 1980s will make*
*it possible to realize the potential of such planning in the 1990s.*

# Strategic Planning: The Unrealized Potential of the 1980s and the Promise of the 1990s

*Larry W. Jones*†

In the late 1970s, strategic planning began to have a measurable impact on the world of business and industry. Some larger corporations, in fact, showed spectacular changes, transforming poorly performing organizations into leaders in their respective fields.

At the beginning of the 1980s, higher education took notice of the phenomenon. Some faculty members and administrators became trained in the ways of strategic planning and attempted to apply these principles to problems in the academy.

The initial efforts were made by individuals in business administration, and they needed to sensitize themselves to some of the fundamental differences between functioning in a corporate environment and functioning in the more academically oriented settings of colleges and universities. Soon, however, the movement began in earnest and many institutions experimented with what they thought were strategic planning processes.

While some programs met with modest success, others foundered on the shoals of misunderstanding and suffered from the absence of insight. Consultants in the field of strategic planning flourished and were called upon regularly to salvage efforts gone awry at large and small institutions alike.

## Unfulfilled Promise

Near the end of the 1980s, it became abundantly clear that strategic planning was not living up to its promise. For every three colleges and universities that initiated a planning process, two soon fell away from it and went back to business as usual. Why did this occur? What had gone wrong with the implementation of processes that held so much promise yet did not deliver with any degree of success?

Let us explore some of the issues involved in strategic planning to see if we can determine what occurred and, more important, discover how these difficulties might be overcome in the 1990s. Perhaps we can determine how, in the next ten years, any institution that wants to realize the benefit of using this powerful tool can do so with a high probability of achieving success.

Initially, we need to ask ourselves just what strategic planning really is when all the verbiage is reduced to its essence. For our purposes we can define it as follows: Strategic planning is the process of attempting to accrue resources more quickly than they are depleted. In higher education these resources are students, money, good will, and any other entities deemed relevant to academia. Strategic planning is also the willingness to make decisions in the present that will affect the future. In essence, we are attempting to create the future rather than let it happen to us.

If strategic planning is such a simple concept, then why do so many institutions have so much difficulty with it? As a first step toward answering this question, observe that the definition provided earlier is, in some ways, like telling someone how to make money in the stock market. All that is required is to buy low and sell high. While this sounds quite simple, we all know that only a small number of people consistently make significant amounts of money in this way. The same is true of strategic planning. All an institution has to do is acquire a variety of types of resources at a more rapid rate than it consumes them. As you may have guessed, the problem lies in the process and its implementation. So, in addition to examining the primary reasons why strategic planning is not successful in many institutions, we can learn a great deal by analyzing a process that has been field-tested and proven effective.

## Why Some Efforts Fail

What are the major reasons why strategic planning often fails in settings where most observers would predict its success?

1. *The president does not assume the role of chief planner for the institution.* This is the most important factor of all. The role of chief planner cannot be successfully delegated. The single greatest mistake is to place the process in the hands of staff and then expect the plans to be implemented throughout the institution. Credibility is quickly lost this way and implementation frequently becomes impossible.

Unless the president views strategic planning as important enough to personally lead the process from beginning to end, it has only a small chance for success. Generally speaking, planning should not even begin until the president is firmly committed to a lead role.

One definition of leadership is "doing the right things." In other words, the hallmark of an effective leader is the ability to create a commonly held vision for the institution and to translate it into reality. Staff cannot do this. They are not the focal point for the various important constituencies of the university. Having them take the point on strategic planning sends the wrong message throughout the institution.

2. *Those directly involved in the planning process do not receive the training required for successful implementation of the plans.* If individuals do not see the "big picture," it is difficult for them to understand the importance of their overall effort. Ego involvement is a function of several factors, not the least of which is understanding. From understanding comes commitment and a dedication to successful completion of the task. If time, effort, and resources are invested in the planning process, the staff quickly comes to understand that the project is important to the future of the institution.

Any college or university that considers a planning process should weigh whether or not it is prepared to make the investment necessary to provide adequate training to those who will be directly involved in the process. If the answer is either "no" or "perhaps," then strategic planning should not be pursued, since the level of commitment required for success does not yet exist.

3. *The trustees and other important stakeholders have not placed their stamp of approval on the process.* In order to fully institutionalize the strategic planning process, the governing body must not only endorse the concept but also enthusiastically embrace it as the means by which the future direction of the university will be determined. In many institutions strategic planning is used as a cover to allow a handful of individuals to do as they please under the guise of shared governance and meaningful participation by a broad range of constituents.

Only when all of the key stakeholders of the institution are ego-involved in the process of strategic planning is it likely to be successful. This type of commitment to the institution is essential and is what a talented leader can be expected to develop among the governing body. If it does not exist and cannot be developed, then the institution is not prepared to launch the planning process.

4. *The timetable established for achieving results is too long.* As human beings, we desire relatively immediate gratification. Even those who have learned to defer gratification have a finite period of time during which they can sustain interest in an activity without reinforcement. A common and serious mistake is to set a timetable of many months or even years for reaching the point of developing and implementing a strategic plan. The needed momentum cannot be sustained across such extended durations. Enthusiasm wanes and, once that occurs, cannot be easily recaptured. It is

far better to capitalize on the initial excitement generated by the announce-
ment of a planning process and set a deadline for results that is achievable
by the participants.

We need to remind ourselves regularly that strategic planning does
not require precise data but rather an understanding of trends and directions. Often strategic planning in institutions of higher education is run
aground by the perceived need for exact information. We must learn to
resist this impulse. Interminable meetings held to endlessly sift through
mounds of lifeless data rank among the surest of ways to guarantee the
failure of the process.

5. *The faculty, staff, and others who will be affected by the planning process
are not provided with a comprehensive overview that allows them to understand
what the institution is trying to achieve.* For planning to be successful, the
faculty, staff, and other primary stakeholders need to have a clear idea of
what is going on and why. Poor information exchange leads to misunderstanding and resistance. Nothing is more difficult to acquire than credibility
and nothing is easier to lose.

One test of the level of understanding is to speak to five to ten faculty
and staff members about the ongoing planning process. A few well-chosen
questions can quickly determine the extent to which these individuals are
familiar with what is going on. It is frequently the case that many persons
are not even aware that the institution is engaged in a planning effort. In
such situations, the process typically entails, in a few months' time, a call
for help to consultants or an abandonment of the effort altogether.

## Why Other Efforts Succeed

Now that we have examined five common reasons why strategic planning
often fails, it is instructive to examine situations in which the process is
successful.

1. *The effort to initiate strategic planning is spearheaded by the chief executive officer.* Where planning has been successful, there is almost always a
president with a vision. Effective leadership means that the president, at
every opportunity and in every forum, articulates the vision in such a way
that people not only understand it but also identify with it.

The chief executive officer must be highly visible in the planning
effort. It is critical that all the employees and other stakeholders of the
institution recognize that planning is the number one priority. When this
is truly understood and internalized, they too will place it high on their
lists of priorities. Only then will the necessary "critical mass" be achieved
that is essential to a successful planning effort. Inasmuch as leadership
translates to "doing the right things," successful strategic planning depends
on the president being seen, heard, and out in front. This helps the stake-

holders coalesce around the issues, which is so essential to establishing and maintaining their support.

2. *An experienced consultant is engaged at the beginning of the process.* The old adage "a prophet in his own land without honor" contains more than a grain of truth. By utilizing the services of a consultant in the initial stages, a good deal of inertia can be overcome. The reputation of a good consultant lends instant credibility to the process of strategic planning and makes the subsequent activities acceptable to the larger group.

Another important reason to engage the services of a professional at this stage is to avoid as many of the start-up pitfalls as possible. By getting a good start, momentum is quickly gained and the entire planning effort becomes easier. In many cases this individual is also available for continuing assistance on a retainer basis should the principals encounter difficulties during implementation of the plan. A good consultant can also design workshops for stakeholders who need to see the big picture right from the beginning.

3. *The governing body of the institution publicly places its imprimatur of approval on the strategic planning effort.* This event is critical to setting the stage for a successful planning effort. The governing body of the institution, through public approval and official action, breathes initial life into the strategic planning process. They also set the stage for subsequent public declarations of support from the other significant constituencies of the university.

Complete commitment throughout the institution and among the primary external stakeholders is imperative for strategic planning to be successful. Once individuals and groups have an investment in the success of a task, they will spare no effort to see that it is achieved.

4. *A realistic timetable for results is set.* It is the rare individual among us who can sustain a high level of interest in a long-term project that does not have intermediate points of feedback and reinforcement. This is especially true for an undertaking that is not of our own choosing and that does not bring us some direct and fairly immediate benefit. It is thus important to establish a timetable that is long enough to achieve our objective but short enough to maintain a high level of interest.

Some successful planners have made a point of developing newsletters with broad circulations to keep the various constituencies informed on a fairly regular basis. Effective communication combined with realistic timetables can prevent flagging interest and maintain the momentum needed for successful planning.

5. *The institution utilizes a proven planning model and modifies it to fit unique circumstances.* As in any other field of endeavor, there are a number of competing models of strategic planning. Several are well documented in the scholarly literature and have been extensively field-tested. Many others, however, are promoted by individuals who have only their financial self-

interest at heart. We need to always remind ourselves that there is no substitute for experience. Only time and trial perfects a process. The task of strategic planning is too important to the well-being of an institution to leave the outcome to chance. Always check the credentials of consultants and talk to others who have used their services in the past.

There are some common characteristics of successful strategic planning processes. They include the following: (1) an environmental scan that identifies the threats and opportunities facing the institution, (2) an internal evaluation process that pinpoints existing strengths and weaknesses of the institution, (3) an assessment of the personal values of the primary constituencies of the university that serves as a touchstone to reality as the process proceeds, and (4) a matching process for items 1-3 that is carried out by a strategic issues group made up of highly respected individuals on campus and high-status representatives from outside the campus community.

## Beyond the Strategic Planning Process

While an understanding of the strategic planning process is critical to strengthening American higher education in general and individual institutions in particular, it is also important to remember that institutions are composed of individuals who have hopes and dreams they want to realize. Positioning the institution, maintaining enrollments, balancing budgets, and other, similar tasks are important, but meeting the needs of students of all types and ages is a greater priority. Lee Iacocca, the chairman of Chrysler Corporation, expressed the sentiment well when he said that "the nine most important words in the automobile business are 'satisfy the customer, satisfy the customer, satisfy the customer.' "

For some time we in higher education have talked about quality and access as the issues of the 1980s and 1990s. Our most erudite representatives have met many times and debated the relative merits of these topics. The proceedings of these meetings have been widely distributed and read. Unfortunately, the academy has not progressed far beyond the talking stage. How have we manifested our concern for quality? What measurable differences have we made in the lives of students? Have we communicated in any meaningful way to our constituencies that we have a greater level of caring about them than we demonstrated in the past?

These are not merely rhetorical questions. Each of them is deserving of an answer and action. But have we demonstrated our accountability with regard to these issues? Are students of today feeling better about their college experiences than students felt ten years ago? Are they currently learning more as measured by some objective outcome measure?

Let us not forget the taxpayers, parents, students, and others who support our institutions. Do they feel they are receiving a greater return on their investment than received by these groups in the past? How about business and industry? We often hear about partnerships between higher education and business, yet only one dollar out of every six spent by businesses on formal training goes to colleges and universities. This is one area where actions speak louder than words.

Other questions also loom large on the near horizon. Why are blacks attending college in smaller numbers than in the past? What explains their dwindling presence? What are the implications for the future of this nation if this underrepresentation of minority groups continues? How do those in elementary and secondary education view higher education today? Has a new era of cooperation been ushered in or is it simply business as usual? The evidence does not suggest they have a higher regard for us than in the past. As we move into the 1990s, the questions raised here must be answered, and action must be taken to implement the strategies identified.

## Summary

Overall, strategic planning and "doing the right things" can make a significant contribution to the well-being of our institutions. The question is whether we have learned from the unrealized potential of the 1980s so that we can shape the future to our liking.

By examining why some planning efforts have failed and others have succeeded, we can gain insights into the major differences between them. The problems are clear-cut, but their solutions are not easy to find. But there are a few general categories that quickly rise to the top of every list: leadership, communication, involvement, training, timing, and concern for the individual as well as the organization. These "virtues" define success in any endeavor. What is sometimes missing is the common sense to pursue them. We need to find creative ways to change that state of affairs.

*Larry W. Jones was dean of professional studies at Morehead State University, Morehead, Kentucky.*

*Higher education needs planning strategies that will increase quality and productivity and decrease cost in the 1990s.*

# Strategies for the 1990s

*Ellen Earle Chaffee*

Strategists for higher education seek to ensure the vitality of institutions by responding to and shaping influential forces in their environments. Perhaps the only generalization about the overall 1990s environment that would generate universal agreement is that changes, complexities, and unexpected events will continue to increase in frequency.

This chapter does not attempt the daunting task of detailing the anticipated environment for higher education in the 1990s. Rather, the more modest goal is to examine a few key facts about the context of higher education and the operational strategies that follow directly from the challenges presented by these facts. The key topics pertain to the primary resources of postsecondary institutions: students, faculty, and dollars.

## Context for the Decade

The number of high school seniors will continue to decline for a few more years and then begin to increase annually. Whether these increases will translate to higher enrollments at the college and university level depends on whether society prepares and inspires students of color for postsecondary education. Also, faculty will be retiring in large numbers, so the availability of postsecondary education depends on an adequate replacement supply of instructors. Judging by the current numbers in the educational pipeline, the supply-demand ratio is not encouraging.

The cost of postsecondary education has been rising faster than inflation, the balance of trade deficit has the United States in deep economic trouble, and no comprehensive solution to either of these conditions is in sight. Without solutions, the nation will be unable to support the postsecondary enterprise as it now exists; many institutions could be lost and many more radically altered in shape and mission.

Other factors in the environment will also affect resources. For example, employers spend nearly $23 billion per year on formal training, only $4 billion of it through colleges, universities, community colleges, and technical institutes (derived from data provided by Carnevale and Gainer, 1989, pp. 18–19). Without better responses to the needs of employers and lifelong learners, nonproprietary postsecondary sectors will lose a sizeable portion of the adult student market that saved them in the 1970s and 1980s. Whatever positive trends and characteristics one might cite for the 1990s, these crushing, interwoven problems threaten to undermine the supply of students, faculty, and dollars and hence the very foundations of postsecondary education.

The basic premise here is that postsecondary institutions can and must manage themselves according to principles that simultaneously (1) increase quality and productivity and decrease cost in order to cope with foreseeable socioeconomic problems and (2) demonstrate behaviors, values, and attitudes that the students themselves will need to ensure the vitality of their own futures.

## Effective Strategies for the 1990s

The suggestions that follow are not new. All of them are likely to be included in the reader's own list of good management practices. The problem is not that postsecondary institutional leaders do not know how to manage. The problem is that they have been pursuing other agendas. Every example of poor practices in this chapter is real. Therefore, the concluding section examines some reasons why leaders often do not follow proven strategies for institutional vitality.

**Make an Unshakeable Commitment to Improving Quality.** The primary value that should motivate all action is improvement in quality of services. Quality became the catchword of the 1980s in higher education and promises to retain this status through the 1990s, so this first suggestion may seem incredibly trite. Still, what is useful here is the emphasis on improvement and unshakeable commitment.

Improvement focuses attention on change over time. Change can occur only through positive action, and a longitudinal perspective minimizes cross-sectional comparisons. As the assessment movement of the 1980s matured, it came to grips with the necessity of using assessment results to make corresponding organizational changes (Hutchings, 1989).

Assessment thus far has dealt only with learning, and rightly so since learning is the central purpose of higher education. However, equally serious attention to improving quality in other institutional functions is warranted, from groundskeeping to purchasing, and from new-student orientation to career placement. All institutional functions can affect student learning and faculty effectiveness, and improving quality in these areas can also improve institutional efficiency and employee morale.

A major potential barrier to quality improvement is the notion that one must first define quality. Herein lies an exceedingly valuable lesson of the assessment movement: Defining quality is a process of successive refinements that can only be accomplished through actual application. Insistence on a full, consensual, unitary definition of quality before acting to assess and improve it will only tie an institution in knots. No single definition can accommodate either the richness of the term or the diversity of contexts in which it is applied. Thus, the many different ways in which institutions have defined quality—often implicitly and under other banners such as assessment, mission development, promotion criteria, and general education requirements—at best constitute grounds on which to begin improving quality and, in so doing, to gain a better understanding of what quality is. Although no one may be able to respond adequately to the question, "What is the quality in the placement function?" many of the partial answers may have substantial face validity.

The second emphasis in this suggestion is unshakeable commitment to improving quality—the kind of commitment that leaves a decision maker with no viable alternative but to make the decision for quality rather than expediency. Every time a decision maker pursues expedient action instead of corrective action, quality is undermined.

Compensation for one concession to expediency may require ten difficult decisions in favor of quality. The academic vice-president or dean who fails to act in response to a documented report of poor teaching sends a message to faculty and students alike that good teaching is not a high priority. The president who fails to act when an admissions recruiter tells students that the college has an Olympic-size swimming pool, when in fact it has no pool and no plan to build one, sends a message that deception is acceptable practice.

**Let Service to Customers Be the Guide for Action.** Customers come in many roles—students, employers of graduates, research funders, and so on. A person may be a customer for some purposes but not for others, or at some times but not at others. On a personal scale, the secretary receiving a work request from an administrator is the administrator's customer, just as the administrator and others are customers of the work the secretary produces. While "customer" may be an uncomfortable term for many in higher education, it needs to become as acceptable and central as "interinstitutional competition" became during the 1970s and 1980s. Higher education needs to mature from the "find and keep students" mentality of the 1970s and 1980s to a commitment to serve students and society in the 1990s and beyond.

Despite employers' substantial investments in education and training outside of postsecondary institutions, employers often say they would prefer that postsecondary institutions provide the training needed for nonacademic jobs. Like it or not, and whatever else may be in the mission statement, preparing future employees is absolutely fundamental to the purpose of all postsecondary education. The enterprise needs to begin to take employers seriously as important customers.

For a sense of what it means to serve customers, compare the student waiting in a registration line with yourself waiting in a supermarket checkout line. They are analogous events. What is your opinion of supermarket management? Regardless of relative product prices or quality, how eager are you to return to that supermarket? What do you tell your friends about the place? Educational institutions need to be so committed to serving customers that they do not wait for a tide of complaints to force them to correct deficiencies in services.

**Increase the Use of Data and Analysis in Management.** Despite significant advances in the last two decades in institutional research and analysis, people continue to find it difficult to use data and research results in their decisions. They often jump too quickly from dissatisfaction to solution by way of intuition, imitation, and discussion. This is incongruous behavior in what purports to be an inquiry-based, knowledge-driven enterprise. The scientific method is too often relegated to research in the science departments, scholarly inquiry to articles for scholarly journals, and data and information to institutional research offices.

For example, regents of a public postsecondary system of research universities, comprehensive colleges, and community/vocational colleges are pushing hard for common course numbering and universal general education requirements to cut costs and solve "the transfer problem." But the regents have no cost information and little documentation of any problem with transfers.

A major research university has completely revised its Western Civilization program four times in the past twenty years solely on the grounds of faculty dissatisfaction with it. They used no data from or about students. Round five is on the horizon.

A comprehensive university heard about another institution's retention program, which had shown spectacular results. The university copied the program as closely as possible. Its retention rate did not change.

**Develop and Use Data on Outcomes and Issues and on Processes and Behaviors.** The focus of the assessment movement on outcomes and the many intervening steps that yield outcomes must be expanded. Too many institutions have adopted a compliance-only attitude toward data on student placement, for example, leaving them with no real sense of what went well or ill in institutional behaviors that led to job placements, or what happened to students after initial placement. A potentially staggering number of institutions have no idea about the extent of their missed opportunities to collect "float" interest on funds or about the cost in waste, malfunctions, and employee time that accrues to the practice of purchasing from the low-bidder.

In academic areas, some institutions use basic skills tests or biennial achievement tests primarily to track students into remedial programs and away from "regular" programs, which are assumed not to be the cause of low scores. Institutions that follow these procedures are making two grave errors. They are missing key opportunities to improve quality because they are not collecting interim, process-oriented information that would permit them to tie test results to instruction, whether postsecondary or pre-collegiate. They are also penalizing students for results that may be the fault of the system.

**Work Closely and Cooperatively with Elementary and Secondary Education.** Such cooperation is not merely "a nice thing"; it is essential to all three enterprises and ultimately to the nation. Nor is such cooperation to be construed merely as postsecondary educators telling pre-collegiate educators what to do. The track record of both sectors leaves considerable room for improvement.

**Respect, Support, and Listen to All Employees.** This is yet another "self-evident" suggestion to which most people would reply, "Of course I do that." But every reader can probably name at least one colleague who does not. Of greater concern is the extent to which organizational incentives, structures, and processes prevent this kind of interaction. Part of the problem is that employees do not spend time milling about in one large room so that they can bump into and converse with people outside their own departments. While the present suggestion does not recommend such milling about, it does call on organizations to encourage employees to express their difficulties, opinions, or suggestions.

The academic vice-president who wants to keep her or his best faculty members is most likely to find out how to do so by asking them what they want and need—and asking before they are so unhappy that they have solicited competitive job offers. The business officer who wants to know how to cut costs in the accounting office can, but probably does not, ask the people who know where the waste and bottlenecks lie, including the accounting clerks and those who send materials to and receive materials from the accounting office. In both examples, administrators must listen and respond to the answers.

**Help Employees Do Their Jobs and Give Them Recognition When They Do.** Helping employees does not mean telling them how to do their jobs based on preconceptions about right and wrong ways. It also does not mean assuming that they can and will find their own way with no support whatsoever. Rather, it means helping employees learn their jobs and how to perform better, making educational experiences available to them and providing them the freedom to select the experiences they want and need. It means finding and removing obstacles that they alone cannot remove. It means sincere and direct recognition when they accomplish special tasks.

**Foster Teamwork.** Even if a large number of geniuses worked around the clock on contextual problems such as those listed above for postsecondary education and the nation, they could not solve such problems by themselves. Businesses are increasingly finding that effective operation requires teamwork on the job, often with teams that cross departmental and hierarchical boundaries.

Team effort and group problem-solving must become highly developed skills not only in postsecondary operations but also in student learning experiences. Most people spend more time working alone in school than in any other setting of their lives. They probably learn more about teamwork on the playground and athletic field than in the classroom.

Postsecondary education is famous for its use of slow-grinding committee processes, so perhaps this suggestion of teamwork will be the easiest to implement. The following ideas may merit consideration, depending on the institution and the task at hand: include committee members from a wide array of functions or departments; form committees that have a brief, planned life span to tackle specific, action-oriented problems; develop in-house "consultants" who can help committees learn to function more effectively; and offer voluntary short-courses on a variety of topics in group processes and communication.

To summarize, these eight suggestions propose ways in which people in postsecondary education can act on certain key values in their treatment of people and information. Businesses that have operated on these principles have not only grown but also have substantially reduced their operating costs. Briefly stated, their financial successes have come from two sources. First, they have slashed what they call "scrap and rework." Postsecondary parallels include reduction of the number of committee meetings that rehash the discussions of prior meetings, and reduction of the number of students needing remedial courses. Second, businesses have created demand where none existed before by anticipating the future needs of their customers. For postsecondary education, that might be comparable to teaching students what they will need to know in the twenty-first century.

## Barriers to Strategies for the 1990s

Despite the prevalence of these suggestions in the management literature and the extent to which they express commonly held values, the barriers to implementation of these strategies are real and formidable. A few examples illustrate the range of constraints.

First, Americans hold strong and in some ways admirable values that conflict with these strategies. The United States was built on competition; its economy is predicated on it. Cooperation has been an afterthought. Also, Americans tend to reward individual initiative, which carries the corollary that failure is attributable to individuals rather than structures. Winning tends to overshadow level of effort or ethical conduct as a measure of success. To the extent that people behave according to such conflicting values, the adoption of these strategies will require basic cultural transformation.

Second, typical incentive structures direct attention to the short term rather than the long term. Trustees want results quickly, administrators change jobs and institutions relatively often, and institutional problems are severe and urgent. Hence, institutions and administrators often seek survival for its own sake, more so than ensuring that they deserve to survive.

Third, the costs in time and money that are associated with implementation of these strategies are not trivial and are unlikely to yield immediate, large-scale savings. Having already conceded that there are strong pressures for immediate results, this factor highlights the problem of finding resources that seem not to exist. Where does one find the time to talk—and listen—to colleagues in elementary and secondary education? How can the payroll get out if someone in that office is typically elsewhere, furthering his or her education?

Fourth, these strategies require far more candid, nondefensive communication than is often feasible or even useful in current organizational settings. What would happen to a faculty member who told a dean that he felt inadequate as a teacher and asked for help? He might be referred to the faculty development office, and he might make dramatic improvements, but would the dean congratulate him or delay his promotion? And if the groundskeeper with an idea about how to reduce the need for mechanical repairs passed the idea along to a supervisor, what is the probability that she would implement it?

Magical, simple strategies for the 1990s do not exist. The suggestions in this chapter may seem simple, if not magical, on first reading. They are not. Whatever one's personal and institutional convictions regarding strategies for the 1990s, the strategies cannot be effective unless they confront root causes and express values that elicit justifiable pride in all of the people associated with the enterprise.

## References

Carnevale, A. P., and Gainer, L. J. *The Learning Enterprise.* Alexandria, Va.: American Society for Training and Development and U.S. Department of Labor Employment and Training Administration, 1989.

Hutchings, P. "A Weather Report on Assessment." *AAHE Bulletin,* 1989, 42 (1), 13-14.

*Ellen Earle Chaffee is associate commissioner for academic affairs for the North Dakota State Board of Higher Education and associate editor of* New Directions for Institutional Research, *published by Jossey-Bass.*

*Conditions in higher education during the 1990s will lead to an increase in the number of women entering the ranks of higher education and, to a lesser extent, in the number of women in administration.*

# Moving In and Moving Up: Women in Higher Education in the 1990s

*Jean Wilson*

In the decade of the 1990s, colleges and universities in the United States will be forced to initiate a number of changes in order to compete effectively in the academic marketplace. These changes and their effects are likely to benefit women in higher education, mostly those who will be moving into or obtaining initial employment in academe, but also those currently in higher education who seek advancement to department chairs, deanships, vice-presidencies, and presidencies.

Foremost among the crises in higher education for the 1990s will be budget cuts and retrenchment caused by increased competition for a dwindling number of young people of college age. To a greater degree than currently practiced, institutions of higher education will engage in strategic planning and other techniques utilized by business and industry in a concerted effort to increase their efficiency and ability to compete in the marketplace.

So too, the problem of the "aging professoriat" in the United States will grow to crisis proportions during the 1990s. Approximately one-third of faculty members today are over fifty years of age. Attractive early retirement packages are becoming very popular and will lead many to leave full-time employment in colleges and universities. There will be so many openings in higher education that highly qualified applicants will be able to pick and choose positions as they enter the job market. Overall, this "graying faculty" situation will prove a boon to females in higher education. For were it not for the employment opportunities it creates, the problems of budget cuts and retrenchment would no doubt be a death knell to progress for women in higher education. Retrenchment means that newer faculty members, more likely to be women than men, would lose their jobs.

One of the current trends in college enrollments is an increase in the number of female students. Not only do women outnumber men in enrollments but also there is an influx of women into traditionally male fields such as law and medicine. However, the extent to which the number of women moving into higher education will affect the paucity of women in middle-level and higher-level administrative positions is problematic. Even though larger numbers of women will be actively seeking advancement, the barriers for women will increase in number as the status and prestige of administrative positions increase. There is likely to be a gradual increase in the number of women in administration in higher education in the 1990s as more egalitarian administrations develop and the male domination in academia declines. To be sure, a higher percentage of women will obtain administrative positions, but the change will be agonizingly slow, far slower than the increase in the total number of women faculty.

## Moving In

Older faculty were hired during a period when teaching was the main focus and research was not emphasized. Newly appointed female faculty members are likely to be hired with the stipulation that they pursue research and demonstrate scholarly productivity. A rift may develop between faculty members, as increasing numbers of women approach their jobs with fervor and begin to attain success in their writing and publishing.

Sexual harassment on the job will continue to be a problem to many women entering higher education in the 1990s. For perhaps half of the women, the harassment will be fairly blatant, ranging from practical jokes to propositions. Fortunately, colleges and universities began addressing this problem in the 1970s and 1980s by hiring professionals (often in the arena of affirmative action) to establish policies on sexual harassment and procedures for grievances. This intervention strategy will proliferate on college campuses in the 1990s.

It will continue to be difficult for new female faculty to establish themselves, that is, to gain recognition. Young female faculty members will find it especially difficult to be taken seriously as scholars. Moreover, the problem will remain that female faculty are more likely to be employed in non-tenure track positions and in the lower ranks of the faculty. Nationwide, 27 percent of faculty are women. While nearly one-third of the faculty in most schools are women, the majority of these are at the adjunct, instructor, or assistant professor levels. Today, only 10–12 percent of full professors are women. Since most schools require three to seven years in rank before each promotion is considered, this discrepancy between male and female faculty is obviously not going to change quickly. Women in the 1990s who want to reach the rank of full professor will have to obtain the terminal degree, spend the time required to do research and publish, and resolve to work harder than their male counterparts. Some women will achieve the rank; more will not.

## Moving Up

Enrollment trends in colleges during the 1980s indicate that women are using education to enhance their social and career status. Women now earn 50 percent of the baccalaureate and master degrees awarded each year. And they earn 34 percent of the doctorates. In addition, 38 percent of law school graduates are women, 30 percent of medical school graduates are women, and 21 percent of dental school graduates are women ("First Professional Degrees . . . ," 1987). Also, there has been a steady increase in the number of female faculty, to the present level, 27 percent of all faculty (Pearson, Shavlik, and Touchton, 1989).

Moving into higher education requires obtaining advanced graduate degrees, shouldering sometimes heavy burdens with education bills, and often relocating one's residence and family. Jumping through these hoops may enable a woman to obtain a position as a faculty member at a college or university. If she aspires to be an administrator, the challenges become more formidable and increase in number. Presently, women in higher education who are in administration are likely to be in staff-level positions that deal with women's studies and projects, remedial teaching, advising, affirmative action, or similar support programs.

In the 1990s, women will continue to face the same attitudinal barriers in academic employment. Commonly recognized stereotypes and sex discrimination in the perception and evaluation of individual competence will continue to hold women back in their efforts to advance in higher education.

The number of women in senior administrative positions in higher education doubled from the 1970s to the 1980s. Over three hundred women are chief executive officers in colleges and universities, so there is obviously some cause for optimism in assessing women's opportunities to move up into the higher ranks of their college or university administrations. At the present time, however, only 10 percent of college and university presidents are women ("First Professional Degrees . . . ," 1987). Universities will need experienced, competent female administrators to assist in the professional development of women who aspire to leadership roles. These mentors can help female faculty members to become involved in professional organizations, introducing them to professional people in business and industry, assisting them with writing and research, directing them to the appropriate journals for manuscript publication, and so forth. These activities lay the groundwork for development of the professional expertise necessary for advancement in higher education.

Women who eventually become administrators in the 1990s are likely to have demonstrated the following characteristics: serious scholarship, interest in the whole university community, high energy levels, associations with other active, energetic people, effective time management, and readiness to take on challenges and to assume reasonable risks.

## The Challenge of the 1990s

To maximize the number of women entering higher education in the 1990s, remedial intervention needs to be planned and implemented on a large scale. Since many of the problems experienced by women are due to social attitudes, stereotypes, and discrimination, it is shortsighted to restrict intervention to the arenas of women's postsecondary education and careers. Intervention should include measures to assure that boys and girls presently in elementary school and teenagers in junior and senior high school do not succumb to stereotypical attitudes and beliefs about male and female roles.

There is evidence that women who enter higher education in the 1990s will be less prepared than their male colleagues. Research indicates that the education of boys and girls is presently significantly different. The National Assessment of Educational Progress conducted three measures of reading achievement between 1970 and 1984. They found that although girls outperform boys at the ages of 9, 14, and 17, the differences in achievement levels between the sexes diminish over time. Girls stabilize in performance and boys continue to gain in achievement. By twenty-one to twenty-five years of age, males are equal to females in literary and reading abilities (Mullis, 1987). Sixty-four percent of the more than six thousand National Merit Scholarships awarded each year go to boys (Project on Equal Rights, 1987). Males outperform females on all subsections of the American College Test and Scholastic Aptitude Test, and, later, on the Graduate Record Exam (Dauber, 1987). When girls enter school, they are scoring ahead of boys; but twelve years later, when they graduate from high school, they are scoring behind boys. There is an inconsistency when girls make better grades than boys in secondary school but boys score better on the national standardized tests. How do we solve the problem? We must strive for equal treatment of boys and girls in primary and secondary schools—equal education and opportunity are not happening now. Textbook and school materials show sex bias. Research shows that teachers at all levels of the educational system ask male students more questions, give them more precise feedback, criticize them more, and give them more time to respond when called upon. As Sadker and Sadker (1986, p. 514) express the discrepancy, "Whether the attention is positive, negative, or neutral, the Golden Rule of the American classroom is that boys get more."

To increase the number of women moving into higher education in the 1990s, colleges and universities must seek ways to identify, hire, and retain quality female faculty. These faculty members must be nurtured and reinforced. Female faculty must be seen as legitimate, equal, contributing members of the academic community.

So too, women in administration must seek out and provide opportunities for other women. They need to share their survival strategies in coping with the pressures they face. Among the most important strategies are to develop assertiveness in confrontations, develop an understanding of the politics of the academic institution, and develop skills in fiscal control and planning.

## Conclusion

We will not see equality of the sexes in higher education in the 1990s. I doubt that we will see equality of the sexes in higher education in our lifetimes.

Developments in higher education will lead to an increase in the number of women moving into higher education in the 1990s. The factors responsible for this increase—foremost, the "aging professoriat" and the increased number of women seeking to enter the ranks of college faculty—will also lead to a more positive environment for women aspiring to administrative positions.

Certain other social changes are relevant. For example, many of today's college students seem more materialistic and status oriented than was evident in the past. College women in the future will be less altruistic and more concerned with getting ahead. In 1985, for the first time, women college freshmen had degree aspirations identical to men's—19 percent planned to acquire doctoral degrees (Astin, Green, Korn, and Shalit, 1985). Clearly, the number of women preparing for higher education is growing at an unprecedented rate. The new direction for higher education in the 1990s is that women will be "moving in" and "moving up."

## References

Astin, A., Green, K., Korn, W., and Shalit, M. *American Freshmen National Norms for Fall, 1984.* Los Angeles: University of California, American Council on Education, 1985.

Center for Educational Statistics. "First Professional Degrees Conferred by Institutions of Higher Education by Sex of Student and Field of Study, 1981–82 to 1984–85." *Digest of Educational Statistics.* Washington, D.C.: Center for Educational Statistics, Office of Education, 1987.

Dauber, S. "Sex Differences on the SAT-M, SAT-V, TSWE, and ACT Among College-Bound High School Students." Paper presented at the annual meeting of American Educational Research Association, Washington, D.C., April 20, 1987.

Mullis, I. "Trends in Performance for Women Taking the NAEP Reading and Writing Assessments." Paper presented at the annual meeting of the American Educational Research Association, Washington, D.C., April 20, 1987.

Pearson, C., Shavlik, D., and Touchton, J. *Educating the Majority: Women Challenge Tradition in Higher Education.* New York: Macmillan, 1989.

Project on Equal Rights. "Equal Educational Alert 7." Washington, D.C.: American Educational Research Association, 1987.

Sadker, D., and Sadker, M. "Sexism in the Classroom: From Grade School to Graduate School." *Phi Delta Kappan,* 1986, *67,* 512-515.

*Jean Wilson is the chair of the Department of Leadership and Secondary Education at Morehead State University, Morehead, Kentucky.*

*The authors discuss trends in higher education in the 1990s and the planning implications for college and university presidents.*

# A President's View of the 1990s

*Kenneth P. Mortimer, Sheila R. Edwards*

The president of a college of university scans the entire institution and tries to anticipate changes in the external environment. The complexity of such an expansive view makes it difficult to discuss the full range of presidential concerns for the 1990s in a single chapter. Increased faculty retirements, rising costs, declining minority participation in higher education, deterioration in campus physical plants, the need for private fundraising, and changes in student populations are all examples of specific issues that must be addressed by presidents during the 1990s.

While those issues are important, we concentrate here on trends in higher education that will have a profound effect on the role of college and university presidents and on the management of higher education throughout the next decade. First, increased involvement in higher education policy by external forces has renewed the debate about accountability to the public and the need for campus autonomy. Second, concern about the quality of education provided by postsecondary institutions has been the topic of many national reports and there is now a growing expectation that colleges and universities will address the complaints contained in those reports. Finally, the tendency to talk about access and quality as though the two were a trade-off has increased to the point where access is often blamed for the low quality of undergraduate education in America.

Not one of these three trends represents a serious threat when considered alone. In fact, discussions about each of them have been prevalent in higher education circles since the early 1970s. But, the *combined* effect of each may accumulate to call into question whether external intrusion into our institutions has changed the nature of the basic academic core.

## Involvement by External Factors

The major change in the accountability debate would appear to be a return to the many debates of the 1960s about educational effectiveness. It does seem that the code words for the 1990s will be accountability in terms of *educational effectiveness*, which is coming to mean accountability for student learning.

The content of student learning, or the substantive autonomy of higher education, is not an area where external involvement has been tolerated. Hines (1988) asserts that during the 1980s the form of this issue was transformed into an argument about intrusion into campus matters. The argument about campus intrusion will be exacerbated during the 1990s by the presence of activist governors and legislators, the increased concern about the status of minority populations, the assumption that the university can and should support the state's economic development, and the increased pressure to demonstrate the effectiveness of educational efforts.

An increasing number of states have governors and legislators who are actively involved in higher education. Many state officials appear to want to give increased support to higher education, but they are demanding some response on the part of institutional leaders as a price for their support. The quid pro quo may be better plans for assessment, more responsiveness to demands for enhancing the state's competitiveness, greater links between higher education and economic development, or some combination of these factors.

There is also an increased concern about the status of minority populations in a variety of states. We are coming to realize that fifteen years of open admissions, increased access, and affirmative action have not contributed to the progress that we had hoped would occur (Commission on Minority Participation in Education and American Life, 1988). Minority participation rates seem to be regressing, the diversity of faculty and staff on college campuses has not met our expectations, and the gap has actually widened between the living standards of minorities and whites. In addition, the emerging fact of "minority majority" populations is a cause of great concern for a number of public policy leaders in many states, particularly in the southeast, southwest, and western sections of the country. Policymakers are looking to higher education to provide solutions and help minorities move into the work force in larger numbers.

The assumption that the university can be a critical ingredient in the economic development of the state is not limited to concerns about minorities. State governments are beginning to realize what private business has known all along: institutions of higher learning exert great influence on the quality of available employees and provide research that contributes to greater economic competitiveness. A number of legislators believe that this link to economic development justifies additional state support for universities and call for a new era of responsiveness. We are not sure that higher education fully understands what this responsiveness entails and are quite concerned that we might eventually be charged with aiming higher than we can shoot.

Finally, there is new pressure for accountability from the states and the public for higher education to prove or demonstrate the effectiveness of its educational efforts. One of the major recommendations of the Study Group on the Condition of Excellence in American Higher Education (1984) was in support of more effective forms of assessment. Approximately one-half of the states have appointed study groups or commissions to look into educational effectiveness and how institutions can be stimulated to pay more attention to the education they provide students. There are, however, significant dangers to the concept of assessment if states treat it too simplistically.

The point, then, is that increased external involvement represents a form of intrusion that affects the very definition of the legitimate areas of responsibility for the state to control versus those best left to the control of the institution. In effect, the argument is that excessive external involvement inhibits the ability of institutions to perform their academic missions, and to the extent to which that is true, college and university presidents need to engage in a serious redressing of the imbalance between internal and external control.

Berdahl (1971, p. 10) maintained that we must "determine which interferences by the state constitute *necessary* safeguards of the public interest, which constitute marginal safeguards of the public interest, and which constitute actual threats to the essential ingredients of autonomy, perhaps best described as the portion of our institutional life and development which is not within the bailiwick of anyone else to prescribe or control or even touch."

Almost twenty years later, we are still struggling with this problem of definition:

> Few individuals would disagree that higher education needs the substantive autonomy necessary to protect core academic functions, but many cannot define either the limits or the exact nature of substantive autonomy. This obligation belongs to leadership. It is also difficult to define the nature and limits of procedural autonomy, and it is in the area of procedural autonomy where the greatest number of intrusions have occurred and where the greatest threat to institutional freedom exists. . . . Higher education must continue to make its own case in the forum of public policy, because it is in this forum where legislative decision can be made to help restore and maintain the autonomy that is so necessary [Hines, 1988, p. 113].

We agree with Hines that the obligation and, indeed, the responsibility for definition belongs to leadership. Many leaders, however, do not know what they would do with more flexibility or autonomy if they had it. It is particularly crucial for the 1990s that we develop more substantive examples of precisely what would be changed if our institutions were given more flexibility and greater freedom from state regulations.

## Concern About the Quality of Higher Education

During the period from 1984 through 1987, a half a dozen or more reports on the quality of undergraduate education in American higher education were issued. The reports brought focus to a national discussion on the quality of the undergraduate experience and represent an important development in the recent evolution of higher education (Mortimer, 1986).

Some observers have argued that these reports symbolize a shift in national attention away from the subjects of fundamental concern in the previous decades: shrinking numbers of students and declining resources. A more modest view of the quality reports is that some institutions have now come to believe that improvements in quality will enhance their attractiveness to students and therefore constitute a major response to the reduction-reallocation mind-set.

This new concern about quality is based on the belief that higher education is getting used to dealing with problems of decline and resource scarcity, but we must do more than simply survive. There appears to be a growing feeling among faculty and administrators that there is no one future for higher education, but rather there are three thousand futures. In other words, each individual institution has some ability to affect the quality of its own future.

It is important to understand that there is a great deal of commonality among the many reports that describe the condition of higher education in America. The litany of complaints seems to hinge on five basic themes.

The first concern is that students have been prepared inadequately for the college experience. This is expressed by the question of whether increased access to secondary education has diminished the quality of input into postsecondary education (Study Group on the Condition of Excellence in American Higher Education, 1984).

The second concern is the lack of accountability for educational effectiveness. One report argues that there ought to be a way of demonstrating to state legislators, students, and the public at large that colleges know what they are doing and that they are doing it well or poorly (Association of American Colleges, 1985). The same report laments the lack of accountability and characterizes it as scandalous and irresponsible.

The third concern in these reports is that undergraduate curriculum has become incoherent. Some people argue that the curriculum has given way to a marketplace philosophy, that is, a supermarket where students are shoppers and professors are merchants of learning (Association of American Colleges, 1985). By this account, fads and fashions and popularity contests enter where wisdom and experience should prevail.

The fourth concern is the decline in the value of the undergraduate degree. A number of people have argued that evidence of that decline and devaluation is everywhere. The evidence usually cited includes business community complaints about the difficulty in recruiting literate college graduates, grade inflation, and declining test scores.

Finally, there is great lament in these reports about the preparation and reward structures for faculty. Observers charge that graduate education does not prepare faculty members adequately for the profession of college teaching, since it tends to concentrate on preparing researchers rather than teachers (Bennett, 1984). Further, many of the reports cite the fact that the college teaching profession has lost approximately twenty percentage points to inflation in the decade between the late 1970s and early 1980s (Study Group on the Condition of Excellence in American Higher Education, 1984).

We believe that the key to improving quality in undergraduate education includes demonstrable enhancement of student knowledge, capacities, and skills within established and clearly expressed standards of performance for awarding degrees. In many cases, the complaints in the quality reports are legitimate and it is the responsibility of the leadership of individual campuses to develop appropriate responses that enhance student learning and maintain high standards of performance.

## Quality Versus Access Argument

As higher education has come under fire for declining quality, some analysts have pointed to increased access as the culprit. A report prepared by the Southern Regional Education Board (1985, p. 2) states, "The issue of access has dominated higher education since the 1960s. Quality became a secondary concern, in part because the early covenant did not specify standards for the programs to which access should be provided—as a way of extending access to all levels of higher education, faculty and administrators lowered standards for courses, student promotion, and graduation. The quality and meaning of undergraduate education has fallen to a point at which mere access has lost much of its value—the greatest challenge is to find ways that will enable both access and quality goals to be met at the same time for the same students."

Quality cannot be increased by simply tightening admissions standards. We must begin to define quality in terms of student experiences. The problem is that prevalent views of excellence in American higher education do not necessarily reflect what students actually learn from their college experiences.

There are three traditional views of excellence at the undergraduate level (Astin, 1985). The first is the selective view: an institution is excellent if the SAT scores of its students are high, or their high school rankings are high. The second is the expenditure-oriented view: "If you have money and you spend it, you must be good." Heavily endowed or wealthy institutions that have high expenditures per student must be good because they have and spend money. The third is the reputation-oriented view: "We must be good because everybody says we are. Our graduates are famous, we have prestigious faculty, and if you do a national opinion poll, you will find out that we are very good."

It is only a slight exaggeration to say that under these three views of excellence, in order to be excellent, an institution need only recruit bright and highly able and motivated students from stable homes, whose parents have given them all of the advantages that personal attention and good schooling can offer. We believe it is nonsense to lock ourselves into these kinds of views of quality, since they shut out such large numbers of people. Rather, it makes great sense to stress performance standards and view excellence in terms of how well people perform in relation to their potential. We seriously need to adopt definitions of excellence and quality that capture the diversity of experiences prior to and during college.

It is important to be clearer about views of quality in order to lessen the tendency to talk about the fundamental tension between access and quality as though the two were mutually exclusive goals. One of the many challenges of the 1990s will be to develop definitions of quality that reflect the diversity of the human experience and the diversity of college and university programs that exist in this country.

## A New Frontier for Higher Education

As higher education enters this new decade, we can define the limits and the nature of external involvement in higher education. The deficiencies outlined in the quality reports can be addressed. Most important, leaders within the institutions are capable of maintaining high standards while working to provide access to all students, regardless of their economic, racial, or class status.

## References

Association of American Colleges. *Integrity in the College Curriculum: A Report to the Academic Community.* Washington, D.C.: Association of American Colleges, 1985.

Astin, A. W. *Achieving Educational Excellence: A Critical Assessment of Priorities and Practices in Higher Education.* San Francisco: Jossey-Bass, 1985.

Bennett, W. *To Reclaim a Legacy.* Washington, D.C.: National Endowment for the Humanities, 1984.

Berdahl, R. O. *Statewide Coordination of Higher Education*. Washington, D.C.: American Council on Education, 1971.

Commission on Minority Participation in Education and American Life. *One-Third of a Nation*. Washington, D.C.: American Council on Education and the Education Commission of the States, 1988.

Hines, E. R. *Higher Education and State Governments: Renewed Partnership, Cooperation, or Competition?* ASHE-ERIC Higher Education Report, no. 5. Washington, D.C.: Association for the Study of Higher Education, 1988.

Mortimer, K. P. "Beyond the Quality Reports: Future Directions and Alternatives." Paper presented at the annual meeting of the Association of Institutional Research, Orlando, Fla., June 23, 1986.

Southern Regional Education Board. *Access to Quality Undergraduate Education*. Atlanta, Ga.: SREB Commission for Educational Quality, 1985.

Study Group on the Condition of Excellence in American Higher Education. *Involvement in Learning: Realizing the Potential of American Higher Education*. Washington, D.C.: National Institute of Education, 1984.

*Kenneth P. Mortimer is president of Western Washington University, Bellingham, Washington.*

*Sheila R. Edwards serves as special assistant to the president of Western Washington University, Bellingham, Washington.*

# INDEX

# ORDERING INFORMATION

NEW DIRECTIONS FOR HIGHER EDUCATION is a series of paperback books that provides timely information and authoritative advice about major issues and administrative problems confronting every institution. Books in the series are published quarterly, in Fall, Winter, Spring, and Summer, and are available for purchase by subscription as well as by single copy.

SUBSCRIPTIONS for 1990 cost $48.00 for individuals (a savings of 20 percent over single-copy prices) and $64.00 for institutions, agencies, and libraries. Please do not send institutional checks for personal subscriptions. Standing orders are accepted.

SINGLE COPIES cost $14.95 when payment accompanies order. (California, New Jersey, New York, and Washington, D.C., residents please include appropriate sales tax.) Billed orders will be charged postage and handling.

DISCOUNTS FOR QUANTITY ORDERS are available. Please write to the address below for information.

ALL ORDERS must include either the name of an individual or an official purchase order number. Please submit your order as follows:
    *Subscriptions:* specify series and year subscription is to begin
    *Single copies:* include individual title code (such as HE1)

MAIL ALL ORDERS TO:
    Jossey-Bass Inc., Publishers
    350 Sansome Street
    San Francisco, California 94104

OTHER TITLES AVAILABLE IN THE
NEW DIRECTIONS FOR HIGHER EDUCATION SERIES
*Martin Kramer*, Editor-in-Chief